How to
KITBASH STRUCTURES

Tony Koester

KALMBACH BOOKS

Kalmbach Books
21027 Crossroads Circle
Waukesha, WI 53186
www.kalmbach.com/books

Published in 2012
16 15 14 13 12   1 2 3 4 5

Manufactured in the United States

ISBN: 978-0-89024-866-9

All photos by the author unless otherwise noted.

On the cover:
Gerry Leone cut off the back wall of his HO Hunt Paints building to provide a unique perspective at the edge of his layout. Gerry took the photo.

Publisher's Cataloging-in-Publication Data

Koester, Tony.
    How to kitbash structures / Tony Koester.

    p. : ill. (chiefly col.) ; cm. -- (Model railroader books) -- (Modeling & painting series)

    ISBN: 978-0-89024-866-9

    1. Railroads--Buildings and structures--Models--Handbooks, manuals, etc. 2. Railroads--Buildings and structures--Models--Design and construction--Handbooks, manuals, etc. 3. Models and modelmaking--Handbooks, manuals, etc. I. Title. II. Title: Kitbash structures III. Series: Model railroader books.

TF197 .K648 2012
625.19

Contents

To kitbash or not to kitbash?

When I needed a two-story depot typical of those found along the Western Maryland's coal branch to Elkins, W.Va., I found what I needed lurking inside a Faller farmhouse kit (now sold by Walthers as the Lancaster Farmhouse, No. 933-3333). The lesson here is to form a clear image of the desired structure in your mind, then look not at the labels but at the photos of commercial kits. The prototype structure is at Kerens, W.Va.

That is indeed the question, as well as the subject of this book. Like any other aspect of scale model railroading, there needs to be a well-understood method to our madness, a *raison d'être*, before we commit our aspirations to hardware. My objective is therefore to offer guidance on how to recognize good—and bad—kitbashing prospects, and to provide tips on choosing commercial kits or even built-up structure models that can be modified or combined to satisfy specific needs and desires.

Jim Boyd

Defining our options

The first thing you'll discover as you page through this book is that it's an idea book, not primarily a set of step-by-step how-to instructions. Had I chosen to follow the latter path, it would have reduced the scope of this book to perhaps a half-dozen specific structure projects. The odds of finding one that appealed to you would have been slim indeed.

To be sure, there are several kitbashing projects explained in sufficient detail for you to follow along, and quite a few more for which a photo or two and a menu of base kits should be sufficient to point you in the proper direction. But in some cases models I kitbashed years ago are now available in kit form, or the kit(s) I used are no longer commercially available, although an eBay search will usually bear fruit.

Before we get into such nitty-gritty aspects of modeling, however, we'll take time to review what makes kitbashing a viable approach to structure modeling, when it's worthwhile to consider kitbashing as well as when it may not be, and—as we discuss in some detail in Chapter 1—why you shouldn't pay too much attention to the label on the box.

Taking the easy way out?

Some of you may view kitbashing as something less rigorous than scratch-building. I'll do my best to demonstrate to those who may hold this view that kitbashing is indeed a legitimate alternative. It may simply be a placeholder, a stand-in for an accurate model of a specific prototype that you hope to build later on. Or a kitbashed structure may turn out to be a rather decent model of a specific prototype, one that may not need to be replaced any time soon, if at all.

Of course, a kitbashed structure, like many commercial "craftsman" kits, may be solely a product of our imagination and not based on a specific prototype at all. The resulting building may satisfy the entrepreneurial spirit that resides in most of us, an idealized expression of how we see the world or wish it to be.

The drive to kitbash structures may even come from the desire to creatively cash in on the sizable larder of structure kits now residing on our storage shelves by using them to fill holes in our scenery with something more aesthetic than folded 3 x 5 cards that announce, ever so hopefully, "Future site of Danville Lumber Co." or whatever.

Developing a strategy

As readers of my previous books or Trains of Thought commentaries in *Model Railroader* are well aware, I see scale model railroading as a way to replicate in miniature not only the sights and sounds of full-size ("prototype") railroading but also the ways the railroads went about their business. It's akin to war gaming, or even chess with motorized "men." So too should we have a strategy as we contemplate what structures we need to represent carload origins and destinations while adding interest and plausibility to our railroads.

Two hints before we get started: I highly recommend acquiring the Walthers catalog for your scale. No other reference illustrates so many structure kits, making it a primary research tool for the kitbasher. And don't overlook their catalogs for other scales; Bill Neale used an O scale bridge kit on his HO railroad (see Chapter 7), and Rix N scale grain bins are similar in size to the diminutive bins seen after World War II when used on HO layouts.

And note that an apparently discontinued kit may later appear in another company's product line. Review the listings of all popular brands before assuming a particular model is no longer available.

1

Do not read the label on the box!

If you were planning to build a model of a soybean processing plant, would you have looked inside the box of a kit labeled "cement plant"? But as I explain in Chapter 8, most of the needed parts for that structure were indeed found inside the Walthers Valley Cement kit.

It's easy to be misled, even unintentionally. Labels, for example, create expectations. If you find a box marked "Cheerios" in the local super-market, you can reasonably expect to find that familiar cereal inside the familiar yellow box. But such expectations can lead to assumptions that get in the way of the kitbasher. If during a visit to a local hobby shop or while perusing a catalog or website we see a kit labeled as a cement plant, it may never occur to us that there is actually a soybean processing plant hiding inside that box (see **1** and Chapter 9).

"Kit-bashing"?

Before we delve too deeply into the pros and cons of kitbashing structures, let's take a look back at the origins and implications of the term "kitbashing." I credit the term, or at least popularizing the term, to Dave Frary and Bob Hayden back in the 1970s during my tenure as editor of *Railroad Model Craftsman*. Like the evolution of the word "to-day" into "today," "kit-bashing" soon segued into "kitbashing."

I recall some alternative terms such as "kit-mingling," but none caught on. The irreverent nature of the idea of bashing two or more kits together to create something else, much like nuclear fusion, adds just a hint of the whimsy that is inherent in the slightly preposterous notion that we really can re-create the aural and visual dynamics of full-size railroading with our relatively puny scale models.

The late Art Curren gets credit for expanding our horizons when it comes to creative structure kitbashing. He also gets credit for applying the same degree of creativity to the "punny" names he applied to his work; "Frenda Mine" (**2**; see also December 1976, January 1977, and February 1978 *Railroad Model Craftsman*) comes readily to mind. Other classics: Jenerick Metal (June 1996 *Model Railroader*), and Hardley Abel Mfgr. Co. and Perry Shibbel Fruit & Produce (both from the now out-of-print book *Kitbashing HO Model Railroad Structures*).

Prototype-based projects

Scale model railroading has sufficiently broad shoulders to accommodate almost any modeling interest and preference. But for the purposes of this book, I'm going to assume that you're seeking not only tips and techniques for kitbashing models but also guidance on how to make those models more closely resemble actual structures, and on when and why to kitbash rather than use a stock kit or ready-built model, or even to scratchbuild. We will embrace freelancing to some degree, but always with our sights trained in the direction of full-size structures found on one or more prototype railroads.

Frenda Mine was just one of scores of creatively kitbashed structures from the fertile mind of the late Art Curren. It's easy to see the basics: the Freight Station kit then sold by AHM (No. 5831) and later by Tyco (No. 7785), among others, atop Bachmann's HO Coaling Station (160-45211). *Art Curren*

Why kitbash a structure?

Before we can make a knowledgeable choice about buying or building a structure that has a specific role to play on our railroads, we need to give considerable thought as to the importance of that role. Some buildings are what we call "signature structures," buildings that will help to set the stage for the railroad as a whole—the stars of the show.

On my former HO model railroad, the freelanced Allegheny Midland, for example, I modified the term "freelancing" by adding the words "prototype-based." The old saw about this being my railroad for which I make all the rules was quietly retired, and instead I looked to regional prototype railroads as patterns for how the railroad looked and operated in various time periods.

When Jim Boyd showed me a color slide he had taken of the Chesapeake & Ohio's yardmaster's office at Quinnimont, W.Va., I decided on the spot that AM lineside structures would be based on C&O prototypes. QN Cabin on the C&O thus became BJ Cabin on

the AM, **3**, and the C&O's historical-landmark depot at Thurmond in the Mountain State became South Fork on the AM, **4**. These were both signature structures on the Midland Road, and I therefore scratchbuilt both of them to ensure that I captured the prototypes' distinctive features.

A potential downside is that I also painted them in C&O's two-tone gray, so a knowledgeable C&O fan might have become confused as he saw familiar structures with odd names in unfamiliar locations. Perhaps I should have created a unique AM paint scheme, but the operational theme was based on the premise that the Midland Road eventually became an extension of the Nickel Plate Road into the central Appalachian coalfields, and all AM locomotives and rolling stock were painted to match NKP standards. I could therefore have adopted the NKP structure paint scheme, but the NKP also painted its depots two-tone gray. That's why the mix of C&O architecture with NKP everything else seemed to be plausible, but it didn't resolve the

The Chesapeake & Ohio yardmaster's office at Quinnimont, W.Va., set the standard for all lineside structures on my former Allegheny Midland. I feel that a signature structure such as this should be accurately modeled, making it a better candidate for scratchbuilding than kitbashing.

3

Another signature structure on the Allegheny Midland was this HO model of the C&O's sprawling two-story depot at Thurmond, W.Va., now a national landmark. Even though it stood at mythical South Fork, not Thurmond, on the AM, it was deemed important enough to justify scratchbuilding.

4

potential confusion about memorable C&O structures sporting new site names in new locations.

I suspect I was on more secure ground with several models of standard C&O wood cabins, **4** (see also Chapter 3), which I kitbashed from truncated Baltimore & Ohio interlocking tower kits and a lot of Evergreen styrene. These were ubiquitous to the C&O and therefore not closely identified with only one location.

The bottom line here is that you want to be sure to define which structures are of vital importance to the overall character of your railroad, and then to create accurate models of them from kits (if you're fortunate enough to have such commercial support), by kitbashing, or by scratchbuilding. This is not a good place to compromise.

And don't be intimidated by the idea of having to scratchbuild a model. The wealth of wall materials, shapes, lumber sizes, roofing, and detail parts such as door and window moldings makes scratchbuilding only slightly more challenging than building a good kit—and you don't even have to read the instructions!

The supporting cast

Not every structure on your railroad will be a key player. It's a noble, and increasingly common, goal to choose a specific segment of one prototype to model in a narrowly defined era, but very few of us will ever have the time or supporting information to build every single structure to match its prototype.

That Jack Burgess has never purchased a single structure kit for his highly regarded Yosemite Valley Railroad is a remarkable testimonial not only to his modeling skills but also to his drive and focus. We've shared a good laugh at some of the tribulations he has gone through in his quest for accuracy. A lesser modeler—me, for one—would probably have kitbashed a stand-in, but Jack's perseverance has almost always paid off with a highly accurate scratchbuilt model, **5**.

I'm modeling eight small towns and cities in west-central Indiana and east-central Illinois in 1954, and in

Jack Burgess collection

Jack Burgess scratchbuilt the distinctive depot gracing the Yosemite Valley at Merced, Calif., not once but twice as more accurate information became available. Here kitbashing was not a means to the desired end. *Jack Burgess*

5

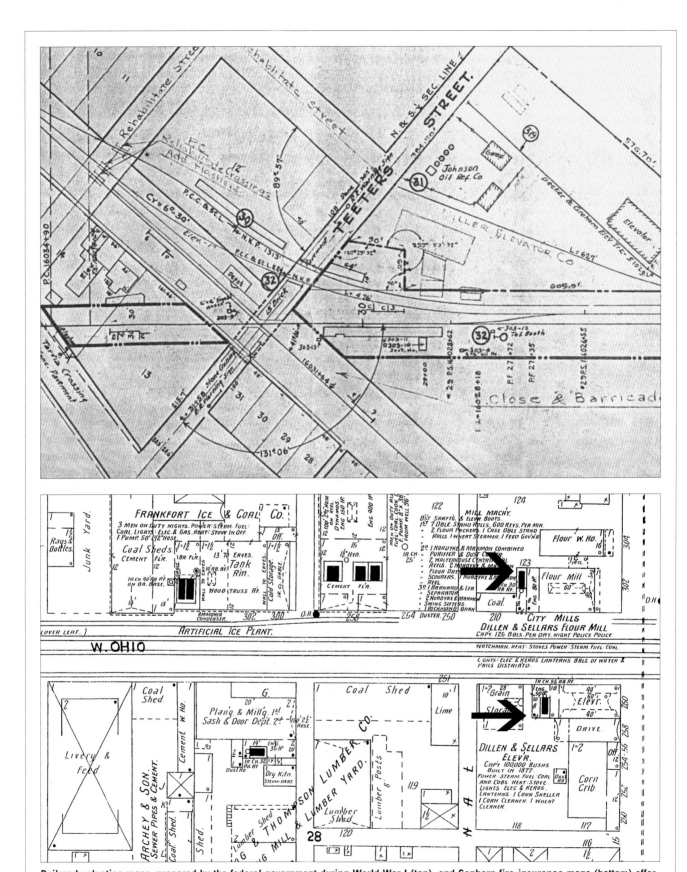

Railroad valuation maps, prepared by the federal government during World War I (top), and Sanborn fire-insurance maps (bottom) offer strong clues as to the footprint and construction of structures. The val map shows part of Oakland, Ill., where the Nickel Plate crossed the Pennsylvania. The Sanborn map shows part of downtown Frankfort, Ind., along the NKP; the black arrows mark a grain elevator and a flour mill for which length and width dimensions are indicated.

A lack of information about an oil dealership in Oakland, Ill., prompted me to paste a photo of a typical facility to the wall rather than try to model it in 3-D. Fortunately, many retail petroleum-products dealers used a fairly standardized set of tanks that closely resemble Grandt Line's Midwest Petroleum Distributors kit, No. 300-5907. *Grandt Line*

7

8

A lack of information beyond the footprint dimensions of a grain elevator switched by the Pennsylvania in Oakland, Ill., led me to use a stock Walthers elevator kit. If photos turn up, it can be replaced with a kitbashed or scratchbuilt version as the scenery here matures.

some cases most of the downtown business districts still exist. But in other towns, the Good Old Days are long gone, and it's very hard to determine what existed in the '50s. Railroad valuation maps created during the teens and periodically updated are helpful, as are Sanborn fire insurance maps, **6**, but in some cases all I know is that a grain elevator or retail oil dealer once resided here, and a bank and store stood over there. Unless photos showing those buildings, say, after World War II but before 1960 surface, your guess as to their appearance is as good as mine.

Fortunately, some lineside structures shared a certain degree of commonality. A retail oil dealership, for example, probably looked a lot like Grandt Line's Midwest Petroleum Distributors kit, although usually with more storage tanks, **7**. That makes kitbashing an excellent approach to modeling both well-documented and almost totally unknown oil dealerships.

Grain elevators are rather distinctive and familiar structures, and American Model Builders, Campbell Scale Models, Walthers, and other manufacturers make a variety of nicely proportioned generic kits. For the long-gone and apparently not-photographed elevator alongside the Pennsylvania Railroad in Oakland, Ill., I picked a Walthers kit, **8**, and I will claim to the bitter end that the elevator there looked precisely like this kit unless someone shows up with a photo of the prototype.

In some cases, I obtained better information about a given structure but still chose to use a stock kit that only vaguely resembled its prototype. An example is the elevator that stood across from the Big Four (New York Central System) depot in Charleston, Ill. I found a low-resolution photocopy of an aerial photo of the Nickel Plate-Big Four junction area, and the elevator's south and east walls are defined reasonably well in the photo.

But on my layout, that elevator is pure scenery. The double-track Big Four main line running between the aisle and backdrop is not even powered, so the elevator isn't actually switched. Moreover, I have hundreds of more deserving projects to attend to, yet that towering elevator helps to hide a hunk of sky backdrop and adds character to the diamond crossing area. So I found a reasonably similar Walthers kit and quickly glued it together, painted it white to match what I could see in the photo, weathered it heavily using Pan-Pastels, **9**, and called it a day.

A covered unloading shed projecting out from the front is beginning to bug me, however, so I may cut it off. But the elevator's subservient role ensures that it is unlikely to receive more intense attention any time soon.

"Good enough"

Allen McClelland coined the term "good enough" to describe his approach to modeling a freelanced Appalachian coal hauler. I interpret the term to mean several things: that the entire railroad is built to one consistent standard of detailing so everything blends in with everything else; that this standard is adequate to convey a desired impression but not overdone to the point that time is wasted on unseen and hence unnecessary details; and that the details and operating practices required to ensure plausibility and realism are not compromised to the point that even high-quality modeling fails to persuade the viewer that he or she is seeing not merely nice modeling but a railroad set in a specific time and place. (See Chapter 10 for examples of Allen's work.)

Dave Frary taught me a corollary of the Good Enough Principle: Don't detail or even model the backs of buildings that no one will ever see from a normal viewing angle. This is especially good advice for the kitbasher, as the unseen, unneeded, and hence unused back (or front) wall of a structure can be used to double the length of the front (or back) of that building, or to form the basis of another structure, **10**.

I confess that I am still a little uncomfortable when it comes to replacing a highly detailed backside wall molding with a flat sheet of styrene or some braces. This discomfiture may stem in part from a brick depot I kitbashed from an Oregon Rail Supply kit into a depot and yardmaster's office for Sunrise, Va., on the Allegheny Midland, a project we'll review in Chapter 2.

"Seeing" the finished structure
Some of you may remember the days of stick-and-tissue model airplane kits. It was challenging to visualize that beautiful biplane pictured on the kit box when you took off the lid and found nothing but a pile of balsa sticks and sheets and some flimsy tissue paper.

The same moment of panic or intimidation may occur when you look at a scale drawing of a structure and then at your supply of scale lumber, structural shapes, and sheets, be they basswood, styrene, or ABS. Difficulty in visualizing the outcome of such a project can utterly defeat some of us.

Again, save for a grainy aerial photo, I found little information on an elevator served by the Big Four (NYC System) at Charleston, Ill., so I dropped in a stock Walthers Prairie Star kit (No. 933-2927) "for now." The stock Walthers assembled interlocking tower (933-2837) is a stand-in as the scenery and track here are developing.

Injection-molded plastic, cast-plaster, or resin kits, or even laser-cut wood kits, are usually far less intimidating. You can see the main components. You can pick them up and arrange them as the kit maker intended, and then rearrange them to see whether they can provide the basis for a slightly or radically different structure. It's but a short walk from seeing the pieces properly arranged to gluing them together into walls and then a complete structure.

You can make scans or photocopies of the walls and cut and paste them in creative new arrangements without risking any of the original parts. Software tools such as Google's SketchUp (sketchup.google.com) let you create "3-D" models of your planned models without requiring a single stroke of a hobby knife or an ounce of solvent.

Scans of kit walls can also help you blend your 3-D models into a photo backdrop. Few models can compare with the detail and texture clearly seen in a crisp photo of an actual structure, but you can substitute scanned images of models to add depth to a scene without admitting to a downgrade of detail finesse.

Modular wall sections
Modular wall sections such as those made by Design Preservation Models (DPM) and Walthers offer many of the same advantages as kits in terms of helping the kitbasher to visualize the end product. DPM offers an inexpensive planning packet of full-size (for HO) drawings of each modular wall section. These drawings can be photocopied, cut out, and taped together to test or conform to your preliminary design.

You can also buy representative wall sections and make same-size photocopies of them. Color copies can be carefully fitted together, bonded to a solid backing, and used as a stand-in for the finished structure. In Chapter 5, I'll show how I used DPM modular wall sections to model a lineside industry.

Kitbashing supplies
Nothing is more frustrating than carving out a niche of time to start a kitbashing or scratchbuilding project, only to discover that you don't have some needed parts or materials. To that end, I do the following:

I keep at least one package of the more typical door and window moldings offered by Grandt Line, Northeastern, and Tichy. I have a package of almost every size of styrene strips, sheet stock, and siding or roofing material from Evergreen and Plastruct. Among many other suppliers are JMD Plastics (jmdplastics.yolasite.com), JTT Scenery Products (modelrec.com), and The N Scale Architect (thenarch.com, which also offers its products in HO).

I also have a decent selection of stripwood and sheet stock from Kappler (www.kapplerusa.com), Mt. Albert (www.mtalbert.com/lumber/), and Northeastern (nesm.com), as sometimes I prefer to use wood to represent wood.

Don't forget the objective

It's surprisingly easy to get caught up in the challenges of kitbashing and walk well past the line where you could have saved time and money, and probably built a better model, by switching from kitbashing to scratchbuilding. It therefore pays to document the steps and components needed to complete a project prior to embarking on what may be a needlessly expensive and overly complex journey with an inferior outcome.

Kits are not cheap, and they're increasingly difficult to come by. The costs associated with producing an assembled structure overseas are not appreciably higher than the base costs to engineer and machine the dies used to mold the parts needed to assemble that model, although labor costs are climbing rapidly as other industries compete for skilled workers.

Assembled structures command higher prices, and despite the cries by some that the lack of kits signifies the death knell of the hobby, the fact that these models are selling well—if they weren't, they wouldn't be produced—suggests otherwise. Indeed, the availability of built-up structures and rolling stock means that we can spend more time on the basic infrastructure of our railroads, landform scenery, and realistic operation, a welcome development in this age of limited leisure time.

But it is easier and less expensive to kitbash a kit than to modify a built-up structure. Disassembling a glued-together building can be difficult, and details can be damaged. Because it's increasingly a fact of life, however, we'll tackle such a project in Chapter 8.

A treasure hunt

One of the most satisfying aspects of kitbashing a structure is identifying the base kit or kits that can be manipulated to create a different structure that is a better match for our current needs. Finding the cannon fodder for the needed building is much like a going on a treasure hunt, and the Eureka! moment when we find the needed kit is alone worth employing the kitbashing approach to structure construction on occasion.

On one memorable treasure hunt, Perry Squier was looking hard for a coal-mine kit that was once ubiquitous but has since been hard to find. We thought, correctly, that the parts could be kitbashed into a tipple seen in photos of the Pittsburg, Shawmut & Northern, which he models in 1923. We went to a large train show and turned the place upside down with no success. But just as we were walking out the door to the car, Perry spotted the familiar blue-and-yellow box with a photo of the tipple on the end.

Perry is the best bargainer I have ever known; he could negotiate a price break on a hamburger at a fast-food joint. But in this case, he couldn't believe his eyes. He asked the vendor how much he was asking for the "priceless" kit.

"$15," the guy replied.

"Will you take $20?" Perry responded.

He paid only $15, of course.

The key to conducting a successful treasure hunt is to have a clear image of the desired structure in mind, and then to utterly ignore the label on the box. As we'll discuss in Chapter 2, the one-story house kits from Rix have a lot of the same characteristics as some Western Maryland depots, especially when you reduce the roof pitch and use a second kit to create a bay window.

I should add a caveat here: It's likely that some, perhaps many, of the kits I used as the basis for the models described in this book are currently unavailable. Few manufacturers order large production runs these days, as inventory is expensive. They are, however, almost always available on eBay, and some hobby shops may still have such kits in stock. In fact, looking for out-of-production kits is what makes stopping at hobby shops during my travels across the land so much fun.

And don't throw away your old Walthers catalogs. You'll need to refer to them when you discover that a kit you planned to use as the basis for a model isn't listed in the new catalog and you need the kit number to find it on eBay.

One last caveat

I really do enjoy kitbashing structures. I also admit that I sometimes become a bit too attached, or perhaps accustomed, to them. Models built as placeholders have a way of endearing themselves, of taking root. Often as not, a structure that is standing in for a really interesting prototype structure that the kitbashed model only vaguely resembles in form if not in function will assume an air of permanence.

Jim Boyd and I stumbled onto a really model-worthy coal tipple at Paintsville, Ky., **11**, and son David and I made another trip down there from our northern New Jersey home to gather more data. It was to add a lot of texture to the Big Springs Junction area of the Allegheny Midland, but I never quite got around to scratchbuilding it.

Instead, I used a kit then marketed by Con-Cor as a gravel loader. Clearly, it was of Scandinavian lineage, probably a product of prolific Heljan, a plastic-model maker in Denmark. As the box-top illustration shows, **12**, he kit comprised two useful-looking structures, and the taller one reminded me of a small coal tipple. I added some additional windows from the parts box, made a walkway out of a length of Central Valley "wood" fence, added a handrail made from another CV parts kit, and removed the cross-bracing to allow two tracks to run under the tipple.

It was intended as a quick-and-dirty stand-in, but there it defiantly stood at

Less than meets the eye: These three photos of Gerry Leone's "Café JTM" show the model standing alone, as it's viewed on his HO layout, and in its "true colors" when viewed from one side. It started as a DPM M.T. Arms Hotel kit (243-119) that Gerry cut down by a full story. The other three sides were used elsewhere on the layout. See more of his work in Chapter 10. *Three photos: Gerry Leone*

These two photos show a two-track coal tipple on the Chesapeake & Ohio at Pikeville, Ky., which was operated by the Dixie Coal Co. back in the 1970s when Jim Boyd and I happened upon it. Trucks from a local surface mine backed up the ramp, were weighed, and then dumped coal into the rudimentary crusher. Great scratchbuilding project, eh?

The box-top illustration showed a gravel loading facility for trucks, but I saw the bones of a coal tipple in the box, another example of ignoring the label. I added some windows, a walkway, an Atlas shanty at one end, the kit's conveyor, and a Life-Like passenger waiting shed for the dump-pit covering. See Chapter 4 for a description of the tipple in the foreground.

12

Modeling the Waynesburg Milling Co. and three-footer Waynesburg & Washington's nearby brick station and freight house at Waynesburg, Pa., would be straightforward kitbashing projects using modular wall sections. The two-story brick depot that graced the Western Maryland's Elkins line at Thomas, W.Va., would also make a great kitbashing project. Consider using DPM's Cutting's Scissor Co. (No. 243-10300) or Laube's Linen Mill (243-10600) as a starting point.

13

Big Springs Junction until the day the AM was dismantled. It looked good, but it wasn't nearly as, well, "interesting" as a scratchbuilt model of the Dixie Coal Co. structure would have been. But I had other priorities—an entire basement full of railroad to build and get operational.

It now haunts a friend's railroad, a stand-in for yet another structure I'm sure he'll one day get around to scratchbuilding. Without a doubt. Probably.

The lesson I learned is to weigh the consequences of kitbashing a little more carefully before embarking on a project. Had I merely knocked together a commercial kit in an evening as a stand-in, there would be no

harm, no foul. But the time I spent gathering suitable parts and then creating a stand-in was a good percentage of the time I should have spent scratchbuilding an accurate, more rewarding model.

Homework assignment

The Waynesburg Milling Co., and the passenger station and freight house built by the three-foot-gauge Waynesburg & Washington (later Pennsylvania R.R.) at Waynesburg, Pa., **13**, are excellent candidates for kitbashing. Compare the basic wall structure to the modular parts available from DPM and Walthers to get started.

Also consider the Western Maryland depot at Thomas, W.Va., on the

Elkins line. It, too, is a natural for kitbashing. Study the photo, then review the brick store and small-industry kits from DPM, Pikestuff, Smalltown USA, and other manufacturers to find a starting point.

Depots in disguise

Notwithstanding the several examples of scratchbuilt "signature" models we discussed in this chapter, on many occasions kitbashing is an excellent approach to filling a space with a unique structure, often with clear lineage to a specific prototype. We'll begin by discussing depots, some of which are hiding in boxes "obviously" mislabeled as something else, in Chapter 2.

1A

CHAPTER TWO

Depots in disguise

To capture the look of the Nickel Plate Road depot shown on the opposite page, I decided the Walthers Pella depot (No. 933-2831) makes a good stand-in.

We all know a depot when we see one, which is a bit surprising when you consider the astonishing range of architectural styles, sizes, and building materials used to construct them, **1A, 1B**. But they all have a certain, well, "depot-ness" about them that lets us identify them even when the railroad they served was abandoned long ago and they now reside in a park sporting Tourist Information signs. The lesson here is that we are well advised to base our models on prototype depots or at least to carefully copy their chief characteristics for fear we might venture too far into the *Land of Make Believe*.

A new sign on the right end of the former Nickel Plate Road depot in Charleston, Ill., proclaims it to be a dog grooming and photography emporium, but the truncated freight door (at left), bay window, and substantial roof overhang (not to mention its location along the tracks) will forever mark this as a repurposed railroad depot.

Common characteristics

As a community, we scale modelers have come a long way since the days of a seasonal, sectional-track oval around the Christmas tree. We increasingly understand that railroads' greatest asset is their ability to network across entire continents, and that our models thereof work better when the trains and cars that comprise them have specific jobs to perform.

I find it interesting to observe the consequences of the trend toward greater fidelity not only of our individual models but also of our railroads as a whole. Where I once saw layouts that were essentially showcases of good but unrelated models through which trains aimlessly circled, I now see layouts that are truly representative in all key aspects from scenery and structures to the operating methodology of their full-size prototypes.

One key visual characteristic of such railroads is that they depict the ordinary. Instead of depots that would look most comfortably at home in Disneyland, each more lavishly detailed than the next, there are often a series of

mundane wood-clad buildings of modest proportions that are typical of those scattered across North America, **2**.

Mundane? You betcha! For every ultra-ornate depot with a roof slope reminiscent of Santa's home at the North Pole, there were legions of rather plain-Jane structures at tracksides across the land. The same applies to houses that could serve as props for Hitchcock's *Psycho* or any good Halloween ghost-in-the-attic movie; rather ordinary residences usually painted white predominate.

This will fly in the face of the preferences and tendencies of some modelers, as they strive to create a Brave New World free from graffiti, mosquitoes, fading paint, dirty vehicles, pollution, and presumably the stress of the next political campaigns. Bully for them! Creativity should not be constrained, but long strides in that direction may lead rapidly away from, not toward, a realistic model railroad.

Modeling the exceptional is not my goal and therefore will not be expounded upon in these pages. Instead, I seek to discover how things

were in the era I chose to model, which is the fall of 1954.

Why then? I lived along the St. Louis Division of the Nickel Plate Road from 1951 to 1958. The NKP abruptly retired steam power on that division in July 1955, and I wanted to model fall grain-rush traffic in the steam era. Several favorite diesels—Alco PA-1s and RS-3s and early EMD Geeps—were already on the property by then.

To that end, I am wringing every last morsel of memory of that time and place from my gray matter, and I'm seeking out those who lived and worked there in the hopes they have photos or memories that will add meat to the skeletal framework I have been erecting. As many others have reported, the research phase of building a prototype-based scale model railroad is a large portion of the total enjoyment one can derive from our hobby. Many of them will tell you that more than half of the rewards lie in the research, not the "term paper" it produces.

So it is with structures, and specifically depots. Slowly but surely, I am

Gerry Albers' HO edition of the former Virginian Ry. includes a segment of Allen McClelland's Virginian & Ohio and the New York Central. In typical understated Appalachian fashion, the depot serving Alloy, W.Va.—a JL Innovative Design kit—is anything but ornate. *Gerry Albers*

uncovering sufficient information to allow me to build or kitbash reasonably, and sufficiently, accurate models of each of the seven depots that will grace my HO edition of the Nickel Plate Road's St. Louis Division. This has led to numerous field trips and even a daylong visit to the National Archives Annex in College Park, Md., **3**.

An easy first step

Let's begin our foray into the potential of kitbashing by taking on an easy depot kitbashing project: the Nickel Plate depot at Oakland, Ill. This depot still exists, but it has since been moved and converted into a residence. The current owner was unsympathetic when I asked, very politely, if I could peel off some of the new siding to see how things looked underneath. So instead I have had to rely on one poor photocopy, **4**, graciously sent to me by a fellow NKP enthusiast. Thanks to the Internet, doing the research that supports scale model railroading is no longer a time-consuming, solo undertaking.

It pays to take an hour or so to familiarize yourself with the structures section of the current Walthers catalog for your scale. This will be a major asset when it comes to matching available structure kits and built-ups to a given prototype. In the case of the NKP's Oakland depot, the eave trim and basic architecture seemed very familiar, so I paged through the catalog until I came across the Design Preservation Models Coal River depot kit. This typical-looking depot has been available both as a kit and in built-up form from Woodland Scenics as the Dansbury Depot (No. 785-5023). I've used both, although it's easier to alter and paint the kit.

I have no idea how the west and south walls of the Oakland depot actually looked, as the photo shows only the east and trackside (north) walls. It's safe to assume the west wall was similar to the east end. As luck would have it, however, the mysterious south wall faces the aisle, whereas visitors will never see the well-defined north wall.

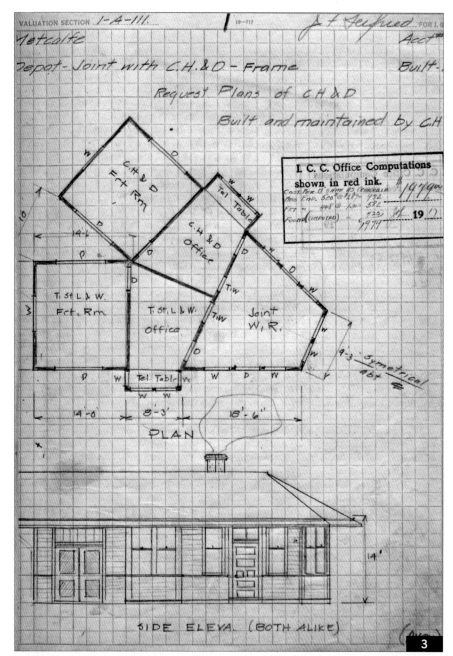

My visit to the National Archives Annex in College Park, Md., uncovered field notes made during the late teens when U.S. railroads were surveyed to determine their book value. Among the notes were drawings of several depots, including the V-shaped depot at what later became the Nickel Plate-Baltimore & Ohio crossing in Metcalf, Ill.

The Woodland Scenics model looks a bit shorter than the prototype, but it's a good basis for kitbashing. I slightly rearranged the doors and windows on the north wall to more closely resemble what I can make out in the prototype photo. If more information surfaces, I can make additional changes or replace the model with a scratchbuilt version. Meanwhile, trains can stop at a rather authentic-looking depot rather than at a bare spot alongside the main line.

House to depot or yard office

Rix makes versions of a handy little one-story, wood-sided house kit (Nos. 628-201 through -203) that is generic enough to be used in several locations on a layout. A row of the basic version can serve as bare-bones rental housing in a company town near a coal mine (see Chapter 4).

The kits' potential doesn't stop there, however. I even found a depot and a yardmaster's office hiding in that box.

A poor photocopy showing the east and north walls of the NKP depot at Oakland, III. (top), is all the evidence that has turned up so far. But it clearly resembles the DPM Coal River Passenger Depot (No. 243-405). The front wall was rearranged to more closely resemble the prototype.

4

The wide roof overhang that characterizes most depots was not a hallmark on every railroad. The Western Maryland, for example, had a number of small depots that looked more like yard offices or even company houses than railroad stations, **5**.

I needed two Western Maryland depots for Glady and North Durbin, W.Va., as the Midland Road had trackage rights between those two locations on the WM's Elkins line. North Durbin was a mythical suburb of Durbin, where the WM interchanged end-to-end with the Chesapeake & Ohio's Greenbrier Branch, and I patterned the depot there after WM depots at Highfield and Williamsport,

Md., as this allowed me to kitbash it from the Rix house kit, **6**.

Many depots and even company homes have relatively flat roof pitches, typically around 30 degrees or even less. By cutting down the slope of the peaked ends and replacing any trim boards molded into the top edges of the original sides, you can make a building look more typical, even mundane.

I therefore cut the roof pitch down to 30 degrees but retained the kit's shingled roof panels. I then cut the three walls for the bay window from a second kit and added the short roof section from that donor kit. A freight door, probably from Grandt Line, was added to one end, a typical feature of

WM depots. This removed one set of paired windows; the paired windows molded into the other end approximated the two separate windows visible on the Highfield depot. A coat of WM's standard gray and deep red paint finished the model.

I also used the Rix kit to build a yard office for the Ridgeley & Midland County, **6**, a short line that connected to the Midland Road at Midland, W.Va. I replaced the roof with sheet styrene scribed and painted to resemble rolled roofing and painted it in the R&MC's standard structure scheme of Depot Buff with brown trim. I should have added window blinds to both structures.

Farmhouse to two-story depot

I needed a second WM depot for Glady. At the time I built the model, I had a photo of a WM depot at Kerens, W.Va., **7**, but not one of the depot at Glady.

Depots located in remote areas such as out on the Great Plains or deep in mountain valleys often served dual roles as the railroad's point of contact with the public and shippers as well as the home of the station agent. This often led to a two-story design, with the upstairs being the agent's residence.

Several kits for two-story depots have been offered, but none that came close to the house-like depots that graced a number of towns along the Western Maryland's remote branch from Cumberland, Md., southwest to Elkins, W.Va., and beyond. As I studied photos of a few of these depots, the distinctive trim piece above each window looked very familiar.

I then paged through a Walthers catalog and found what I was looking for: Faller farmhouse kit No. HO 1130. Unlike most Faller kits, this is a model of a typical American prototype and lacks unwanted frilly details such as shutters that would convert a plain old rural farmhouse into an upscale urban dwelling. You won't find the kit in the current Walthers catalog, but I'm delighted to report that the company's Lancaster Farmhouse, No. 933-3333, is the same building.

Comparing the kit to a photo of a

This is the typical Western Maryland depot at Highfield, Md. Note the lack of roof overhang that characterizes depots on most railroads. *Don McFall*

The Rix one-story house kit (No. 628-201) serves as a good base for a typical Western Maryland depot; a second kit provided parts for the bay window. I used the same kit to build a yard office for the short line Ridgeley & Midland County that connected with my Allegheny Midland at Midland, W.Va. In both cases, the roof pitch was cut down to 30 degrees.

I kitbashed the Western Maryland depot at Glady, W.Va., from a Faller (now Walthers) farmhouse kit using a photo of the WM depot at nearby Kerens, W.Va., as a guide.

7

WM depot showed other similarities as well as some must-change discrepancies. As usual, the roof pitch was much too steep but easy to cut down to a 30-degree slope. Both wings of the L-shaped house were two stories high, whereas the WM depot had a second floor only in the section containing the main offices; the wing seemed to house an attic or storage room.

The double window in the front wall's ground floor was a concern, but a Grandt Line freight door handily replaced it. I found a set of soft-metal castings for a bay window in my parts box (possibly Sequoia No. 135-1009) and stuck that on the trackside wall.

I am very leery of shingled roofs. Too many models proudly sport wood shingles that look like they should have been replaced decades ago and would leak like a sieve. I therefore prefer the molded plastic shingled roofs like those made by Pikestuff (541-1007) and Grandt Line (300-5266) or included in some kits. In this case, I wanted to simulate a rolled (tarpaper) roof, which I made by scribing seams every 30" and painting it with Polly Scale Grimy Black. I also fashioned a small roof for a porch along the one-story end.

As is often the case, photos of the Glady depot, **8**, surfaced later. As fate would have it, it was built to a different plan. I never replaced the original model, but the actual Glady depot looks like an equally good candidate for kitbashing.

A typical country depot

Walthers recently made an inexpensive Trainline-series plastic kit for a typical depot (No. 931-800, Whistle Stop Station). I checked eBay and found several listings for this versatile kit.

With no modification whatsoever, it was an ideal depot for my shortline Ridgeley & Midland County, **9**, and as stand-ins on Perry Squier's HO Pittsburg, Shawmut & Northern. When Perry needed depots for several other towns on the Shawmut, we found that this kit could be either lengthened or reduced in size, **10**, to produce reasonably close models of actual depots along the line.

Photos of the front and rear of the actual WM depot at Glady, W.Va., later turned up. It would also be a good candidate for kitbashing. *Two photos: Don McFall collection*

8

The main lesson to take away from these examples is that a rather ordinary model can be used repeatedly with or without modification, as it won't attract unwanted attention. Moreover, it may readily lend itself to kitbashing into variations on a theme, which is an ideal situation when you're trying to build architecturally similar depots of more than one size to serve communities of various population densities.

A brick depot for Sunrise

In Chapter 1, I mentioned being a little uncomfortable with the idea of leaving a structure's unseen "back" wall unfinished or even replacing it with a sheet of plain styrene or simply support bracing. My concern stems from the fact that, likely as not, I will later

need to reuse that building in a location where the previously invisible back wall will now be front and center, or I'll bequeath it to someone who will.

Case in point: Sunrise, Va., was a division point on the Allegheny Midland, and I needed a combination depot and yardmaster's office that had enough stature to suggest the Midland Road was a big-league operation. Sticking to my plan to pattern AM depots after Chesapeake & Ohio prototypes, I based the building loosely on the brick edifice still serving passenger trains on the C&O (now Amtrak via CSX) at Hinton, W.Va., **11**.

The model, **12**, which has since found a new home on Ted Pamperin's WWII-era C&O layout, is a modified Oregon Rail Supply Menomonee Falls

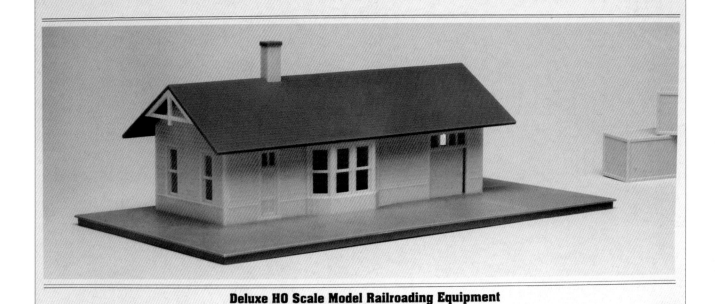

This Walthers Trainline-series kit, Whistle Stop Station, is typical of small-town depots across the continent. It makes an ideal candidate for a freelanced railroad's standard depot.

Depot kit (No. 538-501) that, if built per the instructions, one would expect to find gracing trackside in a major metropolitan area. The catch is that the rear of the depot faced the mountainside on the AM, but on Ted's railroad, it resides in a prominent location where it's readily visible from all four sides.

Fortunately, I did use the kit's back wall; unfortunately, I moved many of the rear window moldings to fill openings in the modified front wall and to create a second story. Since Ted plans to replace the model with an exact-scale scratchbuilt version, the need to find extra window moldings will shift to the next modeler to find a home for the building.

If you compare the image on the kit box to my model, you'll see where major alterations were made. Obviously, the multi-dormered mansard roof had to be replaced, and the central entrance door harks back to the kit's roots as a European structure. I replaced the doors with windows borrowed from the unseen (or so I thought) rear wall and added a freight door and new entrance doors.

I converted the second story into the yardmaster's office. The bay window is a set of soft-metal castings of unknown lineage, but a similar bay could be kitbashed from various detail parts or window castings.

Painting the ornate stone trim brick color helped to tone it down. And molded plastic eave brackets from a long-forgotten source added a bit more American flavor; each bracket could easily have been made from three short strips of Evergreen styrene.

Adapting European kits
I doubt that you'll have a need for a duplicate of this depot, but I shared it with you to point out how it's feasible to modify a structure into something closer to your needs. Indeed, this and other kits' European heritage does not preclude them from being used "stock"

in North America, as Europeans brought their architectural preferences with them when they immigrated to this continent. Certain details such as window sashes may need to be changed, the roof shapes may need to be altered, and some of the ornate trim may be deemed excessive, but many kits from Heljan, Kibri, Vollmer, and others can find suitable jobs to perform on this side of the Atlantic.

Old railroad cars and other structures
Railroads often repurposed old rolling stock as storage sheds, diners (**13**), even depots (**14**). Such cars-cum-structures are among the easiest of kitbashing projects, and the variety of prototypes to emulate is almost infinite.

Depots and freight houses are the railroad's keystone structures, but other lineside buildings such as interlocking towers add considerable atmosphere to a layout, as we'll discuss in Chapter 3.

I kitbashed several depots for Perry Squier's Pittsburg, Shawmut & Northern from the Walthers Whistle Stop Station kit by combining two kits or even shortening all four walls. The small depot at Farmers Valley (top) was made to fit under a Vollmer tile roof molding. Bolivar (above) was kitbashed from two kits with a new hip roof.

10

The former Chesapeake & Ohio depot at Hinton, W.Va., still serves as an Amtrak stop. Hinton was the point where river-grade steam power was swapped for locomotives capable of lugging heavy trains over the ridge into Virginia. The classification yard and engine terminal with its massive coal dock have succumbed to the bulldozer of progress, however.

An Oregon Rail Supply Menomonee Falls depot kit provided the walls for the author's scaled-down version of the former C&O depot at Hinton, W.Va. The kit's mansard roof and clock tower were replaced with a tarpapered hip roof and bay window, the central entrance door became a large window, and new passenger and freight doors were added.

A Branchline paired-window steel coach body provided the key component in this model of a diner that graced the Nickel Plate's yard at Frankfort, Ind., alongside the East Yard office.

13

14

A Quality Craft (later Gloor Craft) NKP wood caboose body served as the replacement (following a derailment) depot at Low Gap, W.Va., on my Allegheny Midland Coal Fork Extension.

Figure 1 (marked with "1" in bottom right corner): A model railroad scene with locomotives and a signal tower structure.

CHAPTER THREE

Towers and freight houses

I kitbashed several towers for the Allegheny Midland from what were then sold by AHM as kits for a Baltimore & Ohio tower. By shortening the first-story sides, building the second story from Evergreen styrene strips, and adding a new roof, the building becomes a close approximation of the prototype (page 33). But consider: This is perilously close to scratchbuilding with built-in inaccuracies, so why kitbash?

Model manufacturers and importers have done a magnificent job of providing us with a variety of structure kits and built-up models, many of them based on actual prototypes. If we can find buildings that precisely match our needs, that's most helpful. If not, we have some decisions to make. We can make do by using a stock commercial structure as-is or perhaps by repainting in our railroad's company colors. The incurred risk is that visitors may see it for what it is rather than as representing the prototype structure that really belongs there. Or we can modify—*disguise*—it to some degree, 1.

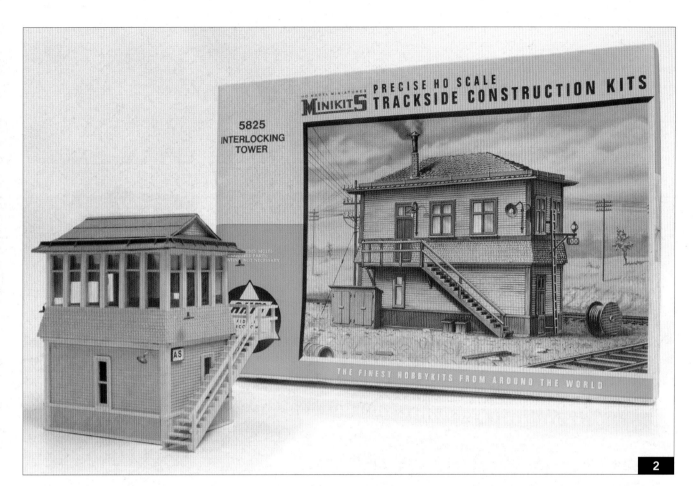

5825 INTERLOCKING TOWER

HO MODEL MINIATURES MINIKITS — PRECISE HO SCALE TRACKSIDE CONSTRUCTION KITS

THE FINEST HOBBYKITS FROM AROUND THE WORLD

2

A cabin of C&O design

I submit that it's easier to visualize, say, an interlocking tower when you open a plastic kit for such a tower than it is to form a mental image of the desired end product by looking at a pile of raw materials. So when I needed several wood interlocking towers that looked like Chesapeake & Ohio "cabins" (C&O-speak for "tower"), I rummaged through my stock of kits to see if I could find some inspiration there.

Voila! I came across several boxes that each contained, the label assured me, an authentic model of a Baltimore & Ohio two-story wood interlocking tower, **2**. Associated Hobby Manufacturers (AHM) originally sold it as kit No. 5825, and Tyco (No. 7773) and others also sold it; it's easy to find on eBay. It is too long, has the wrong style of roof, and the external stairs come down in the wrong place by C&O standards. But, hey, it looked like a tower. The question was whether it could be modified to look like a cabin.

By comparing the kit to photos of C&O's NI Cabin at Prince, W.Va., **3**,

3

The prototype for the cabin kitbashing project was the standard C&O wood cabin such as this example at Prince, W.Va. Laser kits for this series of structures are now available.

D.J. Mulhearn

Charlotte Miller collection

An eastbound coal drag passes the standard C&O brick cabin at Alleghany, Va., on May 28, 1988 (left). I used an Atlas signal tower and some leftover parts to kitbash a reasonable facsimile (right).

4

The tower that guarded the NKP-Chicago & Eastern Illinois crossing at Cayuga, Ind. (left), stood until 1959. A Walthers tower kit (above; stock version at left) provided the bones for the model, with relocated and modified walls and new stairs and roof.

5

The Allegheny Midland's freight house at Run Junction, W.Va., was an easy combination of two AHM freight-house kits (since offered by other firms). The poorly made windows were replaced with Grandt Line parts after the openings were enlarged to accommodate them. The slope of the second-story roof was reduced to match the lower portion and new tarpaper-covered roofs applied.

6

I began to pick out the good points that countered the bad ones. The roof and indeed the entire second story had to go, and the walls had to be shortened, but by squinting just so, I could see a C&O cabin emerging from the kit parts.

I sawed off everything above the band of shingles at a point 9'-6" below the top edge of the walls and discarded the roof. I then cut off one end of the long walls so as to center the remaining window, making them 19'-0" long. The end walls were reduced to 13'-0" in length.

The top-floor window posts are simply T-sections built from Evergreen styrene strips. Siding from the trimmed-off walls was fitted around a Grandt Line No. 300-5088 door to form the back wall.

I patterned the new roof from drawings that appeared in the May 1981 *Railroad Model Craftsman*, slightly modifying them to fit the dimensions of the kit walls. I made the roof from basswood and glued down strips of thin paper to represent rolled roofing, glued on strips of styrene that the C&O used in lieu of gutters, and painted it grimy black. If I were doing it again, I would use styrene and simply scribe in the tarpaper edge lines.

The chimney is a soft-metal casting, probably from Timberline. I modified the stairs slightly to fit the new configuration.

I painted the cabin in standard C&O two-tone gray. Pactra F9 Flat Battleship Gray matched paint chips for the main walls I obtained from field trips, and Pactra M13 Camouflage Gray matched the trim. Scalecoat produced structure colors for the C&O Historical Society (www.cohs.org) many years ago, but any warm (that is, slightly green) medium and light gray hues will come close.

I'm happy with the results, but it's now apparent that only a little more effort would have been required to scratchbuild the entire structure from Evergreen siding and strip materials.

A brick C&O tower

The C&O also had standard-design brick cabins, 4. Walthers has recently introduced a Pennsylvania tower (No. 933-2982) that comes very close to the standard C&O design, and Alkem Models now has both N and HO scale kits for this cabin. Ah, these are good times to be a model railroader!

Years ago, when such variety was at best a dream, I wanted to kitbash a brick cabin that came close to the C&O design. I started with an Atlas Signal Tower kit (No. 150-704). I retained the roof and front wall but extended the bricks on the two-story side wall by using some leftover parts from a DPM kit and made a bay window from the Atlas second-story parts.

I doubt that you'd follow my example today, but it does illustrate the marked difference one can achieve by rearranging kit parts and combining them with leftover parts from other projects.

Cayuga Tower

I had agreed to host friends from distant places as part of a series of operating sessions on several local layouts, and as usual I found myself hustling to fill some voids in the scenery. I had wrapped photos of the depot in my former hometown, Cayuga, Ind., around a block of Styrofoam and was using a stock Walthers built-up (No. 933-2839) for the interlocking tower located diagonally across the Chicago & Eastern Illinois and Nickel Plate Road diamonds from the depot, 5.

I spent a lot of time in this tower as a pre-teen, most of it trying to "help" the towerman move the armstrong levers to line a switch or close a derail. He could do it with the flick of a hand; I could barely move even the easy ones using two arms and two feet. Surely I could do better for such a signature structure, even for the short run.

After years of fruitless looking, I finally received a photo of the west wall of the tower from a fellow NKP fan. But it shows the tower at a much earlier period than I'm modeling, and I know some of the north-wall windows were later boarded up. Perhaps some of the west-facing windows were too. I'm also not sure how the tower was painted in 1954. I have a photo with a 1955 Chevy in the foreground that shows it painted white, and another one dating to around 1950 that shows it with a dark (gray?) trim. Neither qualifies as definitive for 1954.

Bottom line: I'm not yet ready to scratchbuild a model with a detailed interior. Could I come up with a decent stand-in by kitbashing?

The Walthers tower, available at one time as both as a kit and a built-up structure, resembles Cayuga Tower. I

Two Campbell DeWitt's Depository kits were combined to create a longer structure to serve as a freight house for the shortline Ridgeley & Midland County at Midland, W.Va., where it interchanged with the Allegheny Midland. Note roof rafter "tails" along eaves.

8

The Walthers Water Street Freight Terminal (No. 933-3009 in HO, -3201 in N) structure kit acquires a different look with the addition of a peaked roof on the two-story end.

was disappointed to find that neither version is listed in the current Walthers catalog, but they're bound to turn up on eBay.

The model is a bit too long, the roof is wrong, the chimney and entry door are located on the wrong walls, and there is an unwanted first-story window. But by swapping end walls, cutting a door into the east wall, making new stairs from Central Valley detail parts, adding a new brick chimney on the south wall, building a new roof from Pikestuff shingled roof panels, and painting the finished model white, I could come close.

Removing the plain "foundation" for the original chimney would have required a lot of precise cutting and fitting on both long walls, and it's hidden behind the staircase and painted white. It doesn't seem to attract undue attention, although removing it and a window on the opposite side would have shortened the model by an appropriate amount.

Close enough? I think the results justified the effort, but I probably should have cut out that chimney and shortened the west wall by one window. That said, if I later want something closer, not much has been wasted.

Extended freight house

Midland Road structures were based on Chesapeake & Ohio prototypes, and the C&O constructed many of its depots and freight houses using board-and-batten siding. When scratchbuilding a model to exact C&O dimensions wasn't warranted—the AM was, after all, a freelanced railroad—I looked for kits that had B&B siding to maintain the family appearance.

One such kit was the AHM No. 5831 freight station. It was later imported by other well-known firms, including Tyco (7785); I found several being sold on eBay. It was based on a model by Rob Corriston, described in the May 1970 *Railroad Model Craftsman*.

Unfortunately, this kit, like so many others, suffers from the dreaded fat-mullion disease: window moldings that have mullions thick enough to serve as structure support posts, which is an all-too-common shortcoming of plastic structure kits. I'm surprised that an enterprising detail-parts manufacturer hasn't produced replacement windows for the more popular kits exhibiting this deficiency.

The good news is that, lacking exact replacement moldings, we can either file the mullions down to more realistic proportions or perhaps enlarge the height and/or width of an opening to accommodate much better moldings or soft-metal castings from Grandt Line, Northeastern, Tichy, or another supplier.

I used two of these kits to kitbash an extended freight house for Run Junction, W.Va., on the Coal Fork Extension of the Midland Road, **6**. I simultaneously got rid of the dormer and reduced the pitch of the upper-

9

The Pennsylvania Railroad built a large enclosed freight house in Steubenville, Ohio, in 1898 that remained in service into 1966. The prototype building was 300 feet long and 80 feet wide. Bill Neale used Design Preservation Models wall sections for the side walls, gluing ten of the large archways together for each side wall—only 200 scale feet long, as the model needed to be slightly compressed. The end walls were kitbashed from blank DPM wall sections butted edge to edge. Bill scratchbuilt new freight doors and the clerestory roof. *Bill Neale*

story roof to match that of the first story by making a new roof from sheet styrene. I joined the two kits at a slight angle to accommodate a curving track at the platform.

Extending a kit's footprint
The combination yard office and freight house shown in **7** is simply a stock HO scale Campbell Dewitt's Depository kit (No. 200-412) that had the first story extended using wood siding and Campbell window and door moldings. It changes the look of the structure sufficiently for it to pass as a typical freight house, one very much like the freight house I kitbashed for Run Junction but with clapboard rather than board-and-batten siding.

I actually used two Dewitt kits to kitbash this model, but that is an expensive way to get there from here.

Siding and roofing material and window and door moldings available from a variety of suppliers will achieve the same result.

And don't forget simple little touches such as eave trim boards and rafter tails on less-finished structures. A thin sheet of styrene sans trim doesn't make a very convincing roof.

The peaked-roof disguise
Adding a peaked roof to a building kit that came with a flat roof is an excellent way to disguise its heritage. Consider, for example, the Walthers Water Street Freight Terminal, **8**, which was produced in both HO and N scales. It's designed to be assembled as a two-story, flat-roofed brick office with a peaked-roof freight house tacked onto the rear.

By adding a peak to the top floor front and rear walls and a new roof,

the original heritage of the kit is easily disguised.

Pennsy freight house
Bill Neale kitbashed a model of the Pennsylvania Railroad's brick freight house in Steubenville. Ohio, **9**, and on page 61. He used Design Preservation Models wall sections to model 200 scale feet of the prototype's 300-foot length. He cut the foundation from plywood and wrapped it with cut-stone plastic sheets.

Earning a living
We tend to admire railroading for its aesthetic virtues and the intellectual challenges that realistic car- and train-movement schemes provide. But a railroad is first and foremost a business, so we need to provide our miniature versions with sources of revenue, as we'll discuss in Chapter 4.

1

CHAPTER FOUR

Coal country structures

I kitbashed an HO model of a common type of coal truck dump using a Rix overpass kit. Steve Esposito built the dump truck from a Leetown kit.

Ever since Allen McClelland and several of his Dayton, Ohio-area friends started modeling Appalachian coal railroads—Allen's efforts date back to 1958—depicting coal country has become very popular. Today, a wide variety of kits for coal preparation plants, smaller tipples, and company houses and stores add additional temptation. Couple that with a wide variety of articulated steam locomotives from compact-but-potent 2-6-6-2s to super-power 4-6-6-4s and 2-6-6-6s built specifically to haul black diamonds from the hills to seaports, coke ovens, steel mills, or power plants, and the allure of coal railroading in the mountains becomes almost irresistible.

Truck dumps where run-of-mine coal is dumped into waiting hopper cars are common throughout Appalachia, including the sample shown here on the Clinchfield (CSX).

Bridge to truck dump

Let's start with a simple project: a truck dumping ramp kitbashed from a wood (plastic) bridge kit. A truck dump on the East Broad Top three-foot-gauge railroad in Robertsdale, Pa., inspired me to kitbash a similar model, **1**, for the Midland Road using a Rix Products rural wooden overpass, kit No. 628-200. Another prototype truck dump, on the Clinchfield, is shown in **2**.

As the photos in **3** show, about half of the kit was needed. I also scratchbuilt the ramp that's lowered to guide run-of-mine coal into a waiting hopper. Central Valley stairs and a coat of grimy black paint completed the simple model, a true one-evening project.

A common ancestor

Those who model coal tipples from the late steam era through the 1960s or later in N or HO scale should send a thank-you note to Walthers for producing the New River Mining Co. coal-preparation plant kit, No. 933-3017, **4**. As the basis for kitbashing coal preparation plants and tipples, it is a crown jewel.

Despite the kit's Appalachian name, the model is based on a prototype found along the former Denver & Rio Grande Western's branch to Craig, Colo. (See page 67 of my book, *The Model Railroader's Guide to Coal Railroading*, Kalmbach 2006.) This means the kit is suitable fodder for modeling coal plants located almost anywhere in North America.

I used this kit to build models of three prototype tipples on the Allegheny

These two photos show construction details of the simple truck dump kitbashed from a Rix wood overpass and Central Valley stairs. The model is based on a prototype on the East Broad Top.

The Walthers New River Mining Co., available in N and HO, is among the most versatile kits on the market. It's based on a preparation plant located along the Rio Grande's branch to Craig, Colo., but is similar to tipples throughout North America.

The big coal preparation plant and underground mine at Summerlee, W.Va. (above) was switched by the Virginian but accepted run-of-mine (cleaner) coal from a nearby mine on the C&O—loads in and loads out. I used the Walthers New River kit to build a condensed model of this plant (below), with the main walls sized to make best use of the kit parts.

This large truck dump (above) was located along the Clinchfield at Trammel, Va., near the Blue Ridge Parkway. As with the Summerlee prep plant, I kitbashed a similar tipple using the parts from the Walthers New River Mining kit. The kit's large wall sections allow a wide variety of different shapes to be made in one piece.

Courtesy C&O Historical Society

The tipple at Republic, Ky. (above) was, as the name suggests, owned by Republic Steel and supplied coal only to the parent company. The walls included in the Walthers New River Mining kit were cut to resemble those of the prototype (left, opposite). Note the open windows.

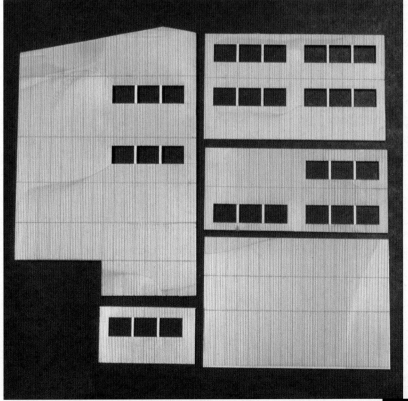

Midland that ranged from the huge preparation plant at Big Springs, **5**, based on a Virginian prototype; a truck dump loader at Trammel, Va., on the former Clinchfield, **6**; and the tipple at Republic, Ky., on the Chesapeake & Ohio, **7**. I also kitbashed several more "truck dumps" from the parts left over from those other projects (see Chapter 1).

I described how I built two of these tipples in the October 1998 *Model Railroader* in one of a series of articles that documented the Allegheny Midland's Coal Fork Extension. If you're modeling a coal railroad, especially one in Appalachia, you may want to read the entire series, which ran from June through November 1998.

Speaking of leftovers: Oddly enough, I discovered that every time I kitbashed something different from this versatile kit, even to make it smaller, I wound up needing parts from yet another kit. The good news is that

you will therefore have lots of great spare parts to build other tipples and structures—after you buy yet one more kit, of course!

A good example of using leftover parts from the Walthers New River kit is the tipple I built as a stand-in for the Atomic Fuel Co. tipple at Haysi (Berta), Va., on the Clinchfield. I felt that the prototype, shown in **8**, was well worth modeling accurately, but I wanted to fill up a bare spot on the railroad prior to a video shoot. So I rummaged through the spare parts box for components to approximate the general layout of the prototype. The office is part of a City Classics Carnegie Street Manufacturing kit (No. 195-109).

Tipple detailing tips

There are a few generic things you can do to make a model of a coal tipple or preparation plant stand out. As you study tipple photos, you'll notice that many windows are typically swung open for ventilation and light, as the glass gets rather filthy in a hurry. Opening the center window in the typical three-window openings in the Walthers kit is easy, **6** and **7**.

Cut the plastic "glass" molding into three separate windows and trim off the flanges around the center window. Brush a thick, wet layer of black paint onto a pane of glass, and press each window molding into the paint to coat the mullions. You'll be able to see that each rib has picked up paint through

the back of the clear plastic. Mount the other two windows normally, but tilt and glue the center window out as though it were pivoted about two-thirds of the way up. Canopy cement, which looks like white glue but is much more useful for modeling (it dries clear, hence is used to attach model aircraft canopies) is ideal for this.

The corrugated siding on this kit does not show the bottom of each row of siding material. I therefore scribe horizontal lines, usually along the top or bottom edge of window openings, **7**, using a dull hobby-knife blade with the blade held upside down.

When I weather the tipple with a lot of water and Polly Scale Engine Black plus a bit of rust colored paint,

Atomic Fuel Co.'s truck dump and loader at Haysi (Berta), Va., on the former Clinchfield provided the inspiration for a stand-in I kitbashed from leftover Walthers New River Mining parts and a concrete-block office from City Classics. **8**

the paint tends to pool along the newly scribed joint, just as soot would do when washed downward by rain and gravity, **7**.

Where to locate your tipple

It's important to understand how hoppers are spotted under tipples for loading. Empties are placed ahead of the tipple, then they roll under it on a slope or are pulled by a cable attached to a winch. The loaded cars are then located in front of the tipple or rolled into a holding yard, **7**. This means that the tipple structure must be located at the midway point of a loading track, not at the end of it.

Empties are not usually shoved under the tipple from the loading end,

as that would interfere with loading operations and could present a safety concern for mine personnel. More typically, a tipple is switched from both ends, and empties are spotted uphill from the tipple so they can be rolled into loading position by gravity, using each car's hand brake to stop its movement. In some cases, an electric winch is used to pull cars under the tipple.

Company houses

"Coal patch" is the derogatory term used to describe rows of company-built and -owned houses that still permeate the coal regions of central Appalachia. They are also found near large industries such as textile mills in other parts of the country; even George Pullman

built a company town near Chicago. They're no longer owned by The Company, of course, but they may be owned by a real estate company that has a remarkably similar name.

Today, you can buy company house kits of various designs, a plus I didn't enjoy when I was building the Allegheny Midland. But the company houses I kitbashed can still add variety to the commercial offerings.

My first efforts involved the AHM Ma's Place kit, which is still available from other sources. It was also marketed with a different front wall as Speedy Andrew's Repair Shop, **9**. I used Evergreen clapboard siding to replace the false-front wall and door, lowered the roof pitch to 30 degrees,

Ma's Place and Speedy Andrew's Repair Shop, from AHM and others, are easily kitbashed into company houses with a new front wall and roof. The bare spot left when the stone chimney is deleted can be covered with ivy.

Dave Frary **9**

and ditched the too-rugged shingled roof in favor of one made from basswood and covered with strips of typing paper painted grimy black. The stone chimney at one end was totally wrong for a company house, but not using it left a bare area on that end, which I covered with climbing vines made from ground foam. Some Grandt Line porch railings and support posts complete the model, save for some details such as old sofas and figures.

Next up was a simple modification to Grandt Line's Reese Street Rowhouses (No. 300-5903). The paired windows are not typical, but by cutting down the steep roof pitch and making a few other mods, and especially by painting them a dull gray, **10**, they'll pass for company houses.

Last up were several Rix one-story house kits, 628-201. The paired windows are a liability and the roof pitch is a bit steep, but otherwise this kit is easy to convert to a company house, **11**.

A company store
The kit box said "store," and I needed a store, but not the typical downtown structure that the kit represents.

What I needed was a large, brick company store to provide a place to shop for the miners and their families who lived in Low Gap, W.Va., on the Allegheny Midland. Company stores are typically big wood, brick, or even stone boxes with large windows across the front and stairs leading up to a front porch, **12**.

This proved to be an easy kitbashing project using two Smalltown USA Hardware Store kits (No. 699-6006), but several kits in this line would have worked equally well. All that was required was to blend in the cornice of the front wall, hide the joints where wall sections were glued together with downspouts, and build a front porch. It's an easy one-evening project.

Coal country churches
A visit to central Appalachia still affords a look at times past: abandoned or repurposed company stores, rows of company houses (often upgraded by current owners), and churches of modest proportions and architecture, usu-

Grandt Line's Reese St. Rowhouses (above) can be converted into company houses by lowering the roof pitch, adding sheet-styrene tarpaper roofs with rafter tails, removing the ornate eave and window trim, and adding "stilts" as required (below).

10

11

The Rix one-story house is easily kitbashed into company houses by reducing the roof slope and adding a tarpaper roof and porch. Most such houses were built in narrow valleys on undulating terrain, so support posts were common.

The repurposed New River company store near Oakwood and Carlisle, W.Va. (top) is typical of the breed with a raised front porch. Such structures are easily kitbashed from a pair of store kits such as Smalltown USA's Hardware Store (No. 699-6006). A downspout hides the joint in the side walls (above). The sign was cut off both front walls and centered. The foundation is from Pikestuff concrete block sections.

12

Central Appalachian churches are often modest affairs with rather short steeples. Almost any church kit can be adapted for coal country use by truncating the steeple.

13

ally of wood frame or concrete block construction, **13**.

Modeling such churches is simply a matter of shortening the towering steeple and omitting the stained-glass windows from a church kit, or kitbashing one from a barn or house.

Where the coal goes

Modelers often focus on the originating end of the coal supply line, the mines and prep plants. But the other end of the conveyor belt can be equally fascinating to model.

Walthers offers a non-operating kit for the distinctive Hulett unloaders that rimmed the southern shore of Lake Erie to unload iron ore and reload coal. Several modelers have already made them operational.

Doug Tagsold kitbashed an HO model of a McMyler Coal Dumper, **14**, which was used at Great Lakes and Atlantic Coast ports to move coal from rail cars to ships from the early 1900s into the 1990s. Doug reports that a few were still in service as of 2012; Sandusky, Ohio, is one location.

Doug models the Toledo Terminal Railroad, and in the post-war years into the 1950s, Toledo was the leading coal-exporting port in the world. There were six McMyler coal dumpers in Toledo: four at the Chesapeake & Ohio's Presque Isle facility and two at the adjacent jointly owned Baltimore & Ohio-New York Central docks. Coal was shipped to automobile plants in Detroit as well as steel mills and power plants lining the Great Lakes.

Doug utilized parts from Walthers single- and double-track through-truss bridge kits, fire-escape kits, and parts from both N and HO scale Walthers overhead-crane kits. The complete model is 64" long.

"My model is not completely accurate or operational," he reports. "But it does provide a focal point for my model of the C&O coal docks in Toledo, and makes it clear why there are strings of loaded hoppers parked in the yard."

Now that we've discussed depots and coal-country structures, in Chapter 5 we'll look at several buildings that could be found down by the tracks.

Doug Tagsold's non-operating HO model of a McMyler Coal Dumper was modeled after the B&O/NYC Lakefront Docks Slip No. 2 near Toledo, Ohio (bottom right), shown in 1981. The other prototype photo shows the adjacent C&O (CSX) Slip No. 2 at Presque Isle; both are operated by CSX today, but none of the McMyler coal dumpers remained in service after the late 1990s. Doug kitbashed it from parts from Walthers HO single- and double-track truss bridge kits, N and HO overhead traveling crane kits, and an HO fire escape, plus a graduated trestle set from Model Power for the approaches, Evergreen strip and sheet styrene, and pulleys made from numerous sizes of buttons and snaps from Hancock Fabrics. The model is 11" tall, 12" deep including the chute, and 8½" wide. *Four photos: Doug Tagsold*

1

CHAPTER FIVE

Lineside industries

Dennis Daniels assembled this modern grain facility in HO starting with a length of 12" PVC pipe for the larger bin and covering it with corrugated panels from several Rix grain bin kits. The short bins on the left are Walthers grain bins built with only eight instead of ten rings; the taller bin is built per kit instructions. He used a Walthers conveyor leg shortened to fit below the upper deck of his railroad; the other legs are also Walthers kits. The office is from the Walthers bulk transfer conveyor kit (No. 933-3519). Dennis built the car-loading platform from Tichy's open grate platform plus Plastruct stairs and handrails. *Dennis Daniels*

The rewards offered by creative structure kitbashing go well beyond the enjoyment of the finished model. When the end product is clearly defined in advance and you find one or more commercial kits that closely resemble key components of the desired structure, it's truly a "Eureka!" moment. Such was the case when Dennis Daniels needed an HO model of a large elevator complex but not one upgraded from the steam era, **1**. The largest bin is indeed kitbashed but not in the usual sense: He wrapped corrugated panels from Rix around a length of 12" PVC!

Looking to the prototype

The Mulberry-cum-Oakley elevator model built by Bill Darnaby, **2**, is a superb example of the potential of structure kitbashing. When he showed a photo of it during a talk he was giving at the annual Prototype Rails meet in Cocoa Beach, Fla., I blurted out "Mulberry, Indiana!" Bingo.

It will serve fictitious Oakley, Ohio, on Bill's Maumee Route, but its heritage is unmistakable to a knowledgeable observer. Bill's Cleveland, Indianapolis, Cincinnati & St. Louis, better known as the Maumee Route, is freelanced. But the care he has devoted to its design, construction, locomotives, cars, scenery, structures, and operation has elevated it to the status of a prototypical railroad, as anyone who has had the privilege of operating on it will attest.

Since the Maumee is freelanced, however, why would he concern himself with accurately modeling a structure that was based on a specific prototype? My guess is that it's both easier—he has an example to follow—and more rewarding, in that he has a benchmark to use to judge its success as a plausible structure.

In Chapter 10, I'll share with you examples of kitbashed structures that are, as well as some that are not, based on specific prototypes. The motivation here ranges from disguising a popular kit's heritage, converting a structure to serve a different need, or maybe just enjoying adding a lot of extra detail and a new footprint to a kit.

Modern elevator

Tom Johnson models a freelanced but prototype-based short line called the Logansport & Indiana Northern in the late 1980s. He had temporarily modeled the line in its original form in the Pennsylvania Railroad era (1960s) but has since been updating it to reflect a more modern era.

One such structure is shown in **3**. You can easily see the original core of this facility is the elevator in the center, which Tom kitbashed from two Walthers Valley Growers Association elevators (No. 933-3096) for his L&IN.

Bill Darnaby kitbashed this grain elevator based on the prototype that still stands alongside the former Nickel Plate Road at Mulberry, Ind. The main building is the Walthers Valley Growers Association, and the brick annex is one of two structures in the Walthers Columbia Feed Mill (No. 933-3090) with a short tower added to the roof. That's a Rix steel tank peeking out at the far left. The storage shed utilizes part of Walthers' versatile Clayton County Lumber kit (No. 933-2911).

Two photos: Bill Darnaby

2

A narrow escape

When you consider a kit as the basis for a kitbashed structure such as a grain elevator, there are two primary characteristics to look for: the kit's overall shape and the materials used for its exterior siding.

The only rail-served industry at Fair Grange, Ill., was a grain elevator switched by the Nickel Plate Road. The elevator has been demolished, but I had taken a sunny-side photo of it on a field trip, **4**. The bad news: I did not think to photograph the "shady" side as well, which is the façade that faces the aisle on my layout. Subsequent field trips have failed to uncover a photo of the east wall.

From what I could see, the building was covered with corrugated metal siding, which made the Walthers Valley Growers elevator kit a prime candidate for kitbashing. I didn't consider this elevator to be a good prospect for

The original core of this sprawling facility is the elevator in the center, which Tom Johnson kitbashed from two Walthers Valley Growers Association kits. To that he added a Rix cyclone and roof vents and a Walthers surge bin (No. 933-2935). The two tanks at left are Walthers corn storage silos (No. 933-2975). The four bins at right are Walthers wet-dry grain bins (No. 933-2937). The walkway was made from Walthers modern conveyors. *Tom Johnson*

I photographed the track side of the elevator at Fair Grange, Ill., but neglected to shoot the east side, which faces the aisle. No matter—the space available was far too narrow to model the actual footprint of the elevator, so I narrowed a Walthers Valley Growers Association kit to fit.

4

scratchbuilding, since I had no idea what the east wall looked like, and I had only a very narrow space between the siding and fascia in which to put it.

Narrowing the kit by lopping off the side away from the siding was an easy task. The resulting model doesn't have the "presence" of its larger prototype, and the mysterious east wall is plain, but it serves the intended function: to provide another source of carloads for my railroad.

For the office, I used Grandt Line's Valley Feed & Seed, No. 300-5911.

Making do

The elevator that was switched by the Nickel Plate at Metcalf, Ill., remained a mystery until I found a poor photocopy of the side away from the tracks (of course) in a crudely produced history of this eastern Illinois community, **5**.

With so little to go on, I paged through the Walthers catalog looking for something that could be extended to resemble the Metcalf elevator. The Walthers Prairie Star Elevator (No.

933-2927) looked like a good candidate, especially since the structure butted up against the backdrop, thus allowing me to use the unseen back wall to extend the structure.

Even by doubling the length, however, it still looked too short, so I used a leftover back wall from a second kit that also butted up against the backdrop. Frankly, it still looks a bit too short, so a third kit may find employment at Metcalf.

Modular wall sections

Using the modular wall moldings made by the DPM division of Woodland Scenics and by Walthers may be stretching the definition of "kitbashing" a bit, but all of the same principles come into play. You first have to identify or conjure up a prototype for the needed structure and then find suitable modular pieces that will allow you to come close to that structure.

Other than a pair of brickyards, one of which made the bricks used to pave the Indianapolis Speedway (hence it's nickname: The Brickyard), the largest rail-served industry in Veedersburg, Ind., was the Globe Railway Equipment Co., **6**. It apparently made castings for various railroad hardware including couplers; my research continues.

Since its day as a railroad supplier, it has gone through a variety of owners. But recently the last owner's sign was torn off to reveal the original Globe lettering created with white bricks.

I saw this as a good candidate for kitbashing using DPM's modular wall pieces, mainly because modern additions completely cover the original track side of the building. I have no idea how the loading doors were arranged on the east wall. I could take good photos of the unseen west wall as well as the front (south) wall, but I could not be sure that the entryway roof was actually there in 1954.

With these loose ends in mind, I did my best to model the south wall from photos, and I arranged doors on the trackside wall to accommodate 40-foot boxcar door spacing. A sheet of styrene, a coat of Boxcar Red Polly Scale paint plus PanPastel (modeling-

A poor photocopy of an old photo (top) is the only information about the elevator along the Nickel Plate at Metcalf, Ill., that has turned up. Lacking sufficient information to scratchbuild the structure, I kitbashed two Walthers Prairie Star elevator kits.

5

colors.com/index.html) oxide-colored pastels to highlight the bricks, and some parts-box detail parts completed the structure.

Expanding the footprint

Back to our original premise: Don't be misled by the label on the kit box. In Chapter 4, two Smalltown USA stores were used to build a four-times-larger company store, and those same kits and several made by Design Preservation Models, among others, can easily be combined to create industrial buildings with a much larger footprint.

I used several DPM Cutting's Scissors Co. kits (243-10300) to create a longer loading warehouse, **7**, for a paper mill at North Durbin, W.Va., on the Allegheny Midland.

Many of the DPM kits are also offered in built-up form by Woodland Scenics, and this may actually make it easier to quickly add an industry to your layout by extending the built-up structure with kit walls. Using very dissimilar wall material may suggest a modern addition to the original building.

Paper mill

Paul Dolkos modified a City Classics Smallman Street warehouse kit (No. 195-103) to create the White Mountain Paper Co., **8**. He removed one of the kit's three stories but added sections to make it longer and wider. The loading dock and canopy on two sides covered some former window openings; others were "bricked up."

The former Globe Railway Equipment Co. in Veedersburg, Ind. (left), which made castings, proved to be a good kitbashing project using DPM modular wall sections (below). The side of the structure served by the Nickel Plate is now covered with a modern addition, so I had to guess at its appearance.

6

Fitting buildings into odd spots

We often need to fit a structure into an oddly shaped space, typically a wedge-shaped area between the main line and the industrial siding that angles away from it to serve our industry-to-be. To maximize our use of such footprints, it often pays to change a building's rectangular shape by angling one wall, thus narrowing one end of the building.

Photo **9** shows an example of this process. A Magnuson cast-resin Menasha Wooden Wares kit needed to fit between the Midland Road's main line and a siding off the shortline Ridgeley & Midland County that provided ser-

vice to the building, renamed the St. George Furniture Co. It now serves as a brewery on Perry Squier's Pittsburg, Shawmut & Northern.

There's a catch to doing this successfully. The angled wall, which is essentially the hypotenuse of a triangle, must be longer than it was when it was parallel to the opposite wall. This means you have to lengthen the angled wall or shorten the remaining wall. I've used both approaches, often by splicing a filler piece at the corner(s) of the now-angled wall or by shortening one or both corners of the "straight" wall.

Neither change may result in a perfect joint, but you can often disguise it by running a downspout along the splices or filler pieces. A climbing vine (just some ground foam glued to the side of the building) will hide almost any joint, **7**.

Another example of fitting a kit to an oddly shaped area is the Atlas Middlesex Mfg. Co., **10**, which has several subtle changes. Paul Dolkos set the far end wall at an angle to fit the available area and added more conventional steps (styrene) and a small loading dock. He also swapped the long front and back walls to better fit the location.

DPM's Cutting's Scissors kits were spliced together to create a long warehouse (right). The one-story end of the DPM kit was raised with sections of brick wall from the unused end walls of a second kit, and the joint was hidden behind ground-foam vines.

Rather than making a structure taller with additional kit walls, Paul Dolkos removed one floor but used sections from another kit to make the White Mountain Paper Co. both longer and wider than the original City Classics Smallman Street Warehouse. *Paul Dolkos*

A Magnuson Menasha Wooden Wares kit was modified to fit into a wedge-shaped space on my former railroad by angling one long wall. An angled wall will no longer reach the end wall and hence must be slightly extended, or the corresponding wall shortened, to fit. It now serves as a brewery on Perry Squier's PS&N.

The four-story portion of this structure on Paul Dolkos' Baltimore Harbor railroad is an Atlas Middlesex Mfg. Co. kit that has one wall angled to fit the available area and the front and rear walls swapped, even though Paul says the kit was not molded to be easily changed. *Paul Dolkos*

Building flats from kits

Although Walthers offers "back-ground" buildings that comprise one wall and truncated ends, it's often just as easy to use a regular kit and to position the front, back, and end walls side by side to extend the structure. I did this with several Magnuson cast-resin kits on the Allegheny Midland at Sunrise, Va., patterned after buildings that once lined the south side of the Norfolk & Western's yard at Blue-field, Va., **11**.

Note that the tallest walls were placed at one end of the scene, and subsequent walls were then stair-stepped down to avoid seeing their lack of depth.

Magnuson's Menasha Wooden Wares kit with its open first story above tracks also formed the nucleus of a greatly expanded American-Standard porcelain plumbing fixtures plant on the Midland Road at Midland, W.Va., **12**. The open wall was extended out from the backdrop to cover the siding and to provide some three-dimensional relief from the adjacent "flats," the two end walls were located on either side of that wall, and the back wall was used to further extend the factory.

Determining a starting point

The industrial building in **13** looks like it was designed to be modeled from modular components. Study the photo, then compare the walls and windows to DPM and Walthers modular wall sections. You won't find a perfect match for the paired windows with the arched top, but kitbashing isn't about perfection.

You can also look for a structure kit that offers a closer match for the pilas-tered, paired-window walls. Walthers Merchants Row III has the needed paired windows and dentil detail but no pilasters, but Walthers modulars have pilasters. Combining them might make be a closer match, but at greater expense and more work. Photo **14** shows such a structure.

Let's move along to Chapter 6 and discuss the type of buildings you would expect to find in a typical town and ways to hide the heritage of the common kits we're likely to use there.

To model the look of the backs of structures that once lined the Norfolk & Western's yard at Bluefield, Va. (top), I used Magnuson resin kits and abutted the front and back walls to extend the structure (middle). The final arrangement (bottom) had the tallest buildings in the foreground with shorter structures stair-stepped toward the right.

11

Still under construction when the Allegheny Midland was dismantled was the enlarged American-Standard plant at Midland, W.Va. I used the rear and two end walls of the Magnuson Menasha Wooden Wares resin kit as flats but extended the front wall out over the siding.

This prototype building looks like it was assembled from modular walls, making it an ideal candidate for kitbashing. The projecting two-story extension at left adds interest, especially if the main building is built as a flat.

Another view of Bill Neale's kitbashed Pennsylvania Railroad freight house (see page 39) shows how he blended a kitbashed structure with stock kits and building flats to create a busy scene typical of Steubenville, O., yet not a building-for-building copy. *Bill Neale*

1

CHAPTER SIX

Residential and retail

A coat of white paint can go a long way toward converting a stock kit or built-up structure into a more ordinary building that can be used several times over. Here an HO scale Atlas house got a coat of white paint and a lighter roof. Two of these homes could be used on the same block without attracting undue attention.

Towns and cities are popular modeling subjects, but they can absorb a lot of modeling time while contributing almost nothing to the operation of the railroad. This is fine for those who are more interested in building models than in using them realistically, but those who view the main role of scenery and structures as providing the context in which the railroad goes about its business may seek shortcuts. And the non-operators among us may want to disguise the fact that they are using mass-produced kits or built-up structures.

A fresh coat of paint

Let's start with a really simple project: a coat of paint. Even a coat of paint may help disguise a structure's origins as a common commercial product. We'll use Atlas Model Railroad Co.'s typically styled and nicely proportioned residence, Kim's Classic American Home (No. 150-613 assembled, -713 kit), as an example, **1**.

I bought two of the assembled versions, but the gray paint and black roof made them appear a bit too "heavy" for a small-town scene. It took me a while to figure out why, and I initially thought they might be too large for my relatively modest footprint I had available for the town "down by the railroad tracks." I finally realized it was nothing more serious than their color.

Look around in most Northeastern and Midwestern towns, and you'll see a sea of white paint. That's the key to modeling typicality in those and many other regions: Paint everything white. I therefore brushed on a single coat of Polly Scale Reefer White, which didn't cover the gray completely and thus gave the houses a less-than-freshly-painted look. After all, only one or two structures near the tracks are likely to have been built or repainted lately. The roof got a coat of Depot Olive.

Note that Woodland Scenics did the same thing with different exterior colors for their Old Homestead (No. 785-5040) and Granny's House (No. 785-5027) built-up residences, **2**. The color change plus a few new details—changes any modeler could have made—lent a whole new look to the same basic structure.

Wedge-shaped spaces

In Chapter 5, I discussed how angling one wall of a structure to fit an oddly shaped space creates a geometric dilemma: The angled wall now becomes longer than its opposite-wall counterpart, which requires the angled wall to be lengthened or the opposite wall to be shortened.

Another example of this is a brick building that housed retail shops in Sunrise, Va., on the Allegheny Midland. I joined a pair of Smalltown USA store kits (any of their extensive line would work) to make the building twice as long, which also helps to disguise its heritage, **3**.

Part of its retaining-wall foundation had to angle in to accommodate a railroad siding, so I narrowed the left end of the building and angled the left half of the rear wall to accommodate the curve. Slightly shortening the unseen front wall accommodated the overall shortening of the building from the angled railroad-side wall.

Altering a structure's width

Many commercial kits have a footprint with a ratio of about 3:5; if it's 5" long, it's about 3" wide. By simply combing two kits into one long or wider building, you can disguise the kit's heritage to a surprising degree, as I illustrated with a company store in Chapter 4. Note that this is essentially what Smalltown USA already did for you in their Appliance Mart, Furniture Showroom, and Rusty's Graphic Arts kits. You can follow their example to expand, and hence change the appearance of, almost any of their versatile kits. A vertically mounted sign or downspout will hide the butt joints.

A simple example of joining two kits to extend the footprint is the roadhouse that Jim Boyd kitbashed from a pair of Revell farmhouses, **4**. Any house kit would do equally well, and the resulting structure could serve as an old hotel, office building, or in a variety of other uses with little modification.

Another example of changing the width of a structure to alter its

Woodland Scenics markets the same basic structure as several different residences simply by changing the colors and adding different details, here Granny's House (785-5027, top) and the Old Homestead (785-5040). *Two photos: Woodland Scenics*

2

Two Smalltown USA stores were butted end to end with the left half's trackside wall angled to accommodate the concrete retaining wall below it. A balcony made from a Central Valley fence turned on its side and leftover roof sections, plus styrene strips, added more depth to the building.

appearance: Note how the slightly narrower store on the left retains the aesthetics of its wider counterpart, **5**, illustrating how selective compression can save space without losing a structure's original appearance.

Abutting the backdrop

In a perfect world, there would be just enough space for everything to fit neatly next to everything else. We do not live in a perfect world; even the miniature world that we supposedly control will throw us curves—or, more to the point, angles.

The railroad I model headed southwesterly from Toledo, Ohio, to St. Louis, Mo. The surveyors who laid out the several short lines that eventually merged into one trunk line were therefore seldom able to run parallel to east-west or north-south section lines. More typically, the right-of-way

angled through fields and towns.

This becomes very evident on my HO edition of this line, as many of the streets cross the railroad at rather sharp angles and continue into the backdrop at the same acute angle. It follows that the buildings that abut those streets will also encounter the backdrop at a sharp angle.

Slicing off the corner of a standard kit or built-up structure to make it snuggle up against the angled backdrop is still a form of kitbashing—the original is modified to meet a specific need. I reused some generic downtown stores salvaged from the Allegheny Midland on my new Nickel Plate layout, and several of those had to endure the teeth of a razor saw as I removed a corner or entire side wall to accommodate the backdrop plane, **6**.

I don't have any idea what the actual buildings looked like in several towns

that I'm modeling. Sanborn maps show a "bank" or "store" and may tell me it was a brick or frame building, how many stories it boasted, and how wide and long it was. Beyond that, however, its appearance is anyone's guess, and town history books have not always been helpful.

I therefore will employ generic-looking buildings unless and until someone comes up with photos of the towns as they looked in the 1950s. So the main objective was to avoid any structure that was an eye-catcher and therefore would tend to attract undue and unwanted attention. Fortunately, several kit and ready-built structure makers produce very plain-Jane small-town buildings.

Narrow spaces

The trend in layout design is clearly toward around-the-walls layouts, often with a central peninsula. It follows that the narrower we can make the shelves on which our railroads and the complementing scenery and structures reside, the more railroad we can fit into a room, and/or the wider the aisles can be.

To that end, I settled on a typical benchwork width of 16", which seemed a bit narrow at the time but has turned out to be more generous than I realized. I could have easily shaved off perhaps 4" from each shelf, especially in the long runs between towns, thus gaining another 8" of badly needed aisle width.

That "generous" 16" of width is not sufficient for some towns because, as luck would have it, the depot where the Nickel Plate crossed another railroad was not only L- or V-shaped but was on the aisle side of the NKP main. I therefore expanded the benchwork to 24" in most towns.

But Veedersburg, Ind., was allocated only the standard 16" width. When it came time to add industries for the railroad to switch, this proved to be a might tight. I described the Globe Railway Equipment Co., built from DPM modular wall sections, in Chapter 5; it came within a fraction of an inch of being too wide to fit between the backdrop and a previously installed siding.

Photo 7 shows another example of a close call. In fact, I really didn't even try to fit most of the needed structures into the available space. Some are simply digital images that I backdated and glued to the backdrop. One lumberyard building is a stock Walthers Co-op Storage Shed kit (No. 933-3529) with the roof trimmed off along the back wall. The lumber storage building is the popular Atlas Lumber Yard & Office kit (No. 150-750) with most of

it cut off to slide between the siding and the backdrop.

I made no attempt to blend the truncated 3-D building into a 2-D image on the backdrop. My only goal was to inform operating crews that this is Veedersburg Lumber, and cars with that destination on a waybill should be spotted right here.

Digital "prototypes"

Most digital cameras come with photo-editing software. You can also buy relatively inexpensive photo-editing software, and one of the most versatile and popular programs is Adobe's Photoshop Elements (PSE). This is a relatively easy-to-use version of the very sophisticated and powerful (and expensive) Photoshop software that professionals use. The latest version of PSE for a PC or Mac costs under $100.

Jim Boyd kitbashed the roadhouse at right from a pair of Revell farmhouse kits, but any two-story frame house kits would work equally well. The same structure could serve as a variety of businesses or as an apartment house.

These two similar stores along the Norfolk & Western (now NS) main line in Davy, W.Va., show how selective compression—the building on the left is both narrower and shorter than its counterpart on the right—need not change the basic look of a structure.

Kitbashing encompasses anything that alters the "stock" appearance of a kit, including cutting off one side to accommodate an angled backdrop. The author uses generic-looking frame and brick structures when he has little information on their prototypes, as was the case for Metcalf, Ill., which is still under construction.

An Atlas lumberyard had to be shortened considerably to fit in the 3½"-wide area between the siding and the backdrop on the author's HO railroad at Veedersburg, Ind. The foreground building is the Walthers Co-op Storage Shed.

I consider PSE almost as handy as a hobby knife. I use it to make signs, create photo panoramas for my backdrops, remove the perspective from photos of building sides or fronts to use as flats in lieu of actually modeling them, and so on.

I ran into an interesting problem regarding perspective on my NKP layout at Veedersburg, Ind. I had retouched a recent photo of Second Street in downtown Veedersburg to remove modern vehicles and signs, 8. This included the front of the Farmer's Co-op building.

But the side of that building could not retain any perspective, as it is adjacent and parallel to a railroad siding. Fortunately, I had photographed it at right angles to the wall and could retouch that photo to remove modern additions. I then glued the flat side image to the backdrop, which created a slightly odd joint where the no-perspective side wall met the "angled" front wall. The same problem would have existed had I used an actual building flat instead of a photograph if I had retained the perspective image looking west up Second Street.

You can use a digital camera and photo-editing software to create backdrops that match foreground kit walls. Simply paint and photograph the kit walls, size and arrange them as desired using photo-editing software, and then print them out and glue them to the backdrop. This ensures that the detail on the backdrop images does not exceed that of the foreground buildings or flats.

Another use for photo-editing software is to retouch a photo of a kit or built-up structure to see how it might look with a different roof, 9, a modernized or backdated front entrance, a different paint scheme, or other modification. You can also digitally photograph or scan the walls of a kit and use prints of those scans to experiment with stacked walls or using the ends and back walls to extend the front wall as a flat.

Bridges are a perennial favorite of modelers, so we'll devote Chapter 7 just to them.

The photo backdrop showing downtown Veedersburg, Ind., was "kitbashed" by backdating a recent photo using Photoshop Elements and then combining that with a flat (no perspective) side view of the Farmer's co-op building. The flat side looks correct when viewed from any angle (above), but the street scene's perspective appears correct only when viewed from a low angle (right).

8

It's easy to use photo-editing software such as the Paint Brush tool to revise a photo—here, to change the roof of a Walthers Merchants Row III kit from a flat to a hip roof—to check the final appearance before purchasing a kit or built-up model.

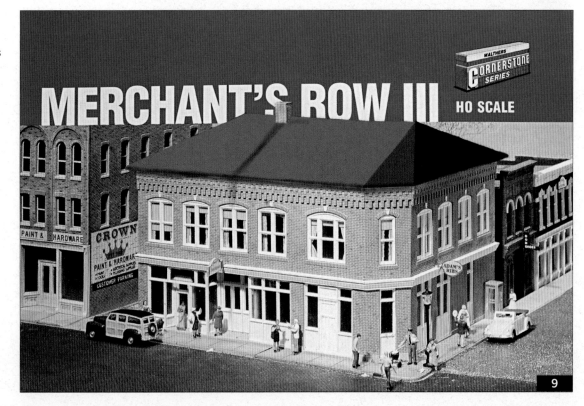

9

1

CHAPTER SEVEN
Bridges and trestles

Ted Pamperin modified a Central Valley through-truss bridge kit to model the C&O's skewed bridge over the New River at Thurmond, W.Va. The prototype is a curved-chord design, which means the top chord of the bridge arches upward. To achieve that appearance, Ted shortened some of the diagonal beams and each end. The center portion of the bridge and the girders that support the track were assembled per kit instructions. Ted skewed the bridge by extending the top chord on one end of each side truss about two-thirds of a panel in length. Both sides of the bridge are exactly the same (built to one pattern) with one side turned 180 degrees. *Ted Pamperin*

Bridges have always been a focal point on model railroads. Thanks to Atlas, Central Valley, Micro Engineering, and Walthers, among others, most of the components to construct steel girder and truss bridges are readily at hand. Our main task is either to create a need that precisely matches the span of a commercial kit or to re-engineer a kit to accommodate a specific need, as Ted Pamperin did for a bridge across the New River at Thurmond, W.Va., on his HO Chesapeake & Ohio, **1**. The latter approach offers far more flexibility and usually allows us to model a specific prototype to a higher degree of fidelity.

"Engineering" your bridge

I've observed many basic mistakes in bridge construction, so it's worth spending a little time reviewing how a bridge works. Short bridges built of wood or metal are beam bridges—think of a log bridging a narrow stream. It has abutments at each end—the stream banks—and has enough strength to support its designed load—a person or two walking over it.

When the chasm is too wide for a simple beam to cross, then a more creative solution is required. The easiest solution might be to run a log halfway out from each bank, piling a lot of rocks on the shore ends to keep either log from tipping over. We could then walk out onto one log and hop over to

the one thus anchored to—that is, can-tilevered from—the other shore.

We could also build some sort of pier midway across to support the outer ends of our two logs. We might even hang some cables from support posts on either shore, anchor the ends of the cables, and then drop additional cables to support our logs, thus forming a suspension bridge. Railroads and suspension bridges generally don't get along, so we'll go back to the simple beam bridge.

If you look carefully at the two general types of steel bridges, girder and truss, you'll see that a truss bridge is actually a girder bridge too, **2**. The trusses, like the cables in a suspension bridge, are there to support the floor

beams or girders. A truss is used when the needed span grows to the point that a girder would become too massive for practical construction and use.

A rough rule of thumb for a girder bridge, be it "through" (with the sides extending above track level) or "deck" (the girders are under the track bed), is that the length should not be more than seven times the height of the girder. So you can't realistically model a 12"-long girder bridge by simply gluing two 6"-long girders end to end. And if you have a 1" high girder, you wouldn't expect it to be more than about 7" long.

A second good rule of thumb is that a beam should be supported only at its ends. You will see old bridges with an extra pier or bent (a wood trestle is just

I kitbashed this deck truss bridge on the Allegheny Midland by combining Walthers trusses with Micro Engineering girders and bents. It's essentially a series of deck girders supported at each end by the abutments, a pier or tower, or by a connection to one (as here) or more main joints on the truss. The truss is supported by two concrete piers.

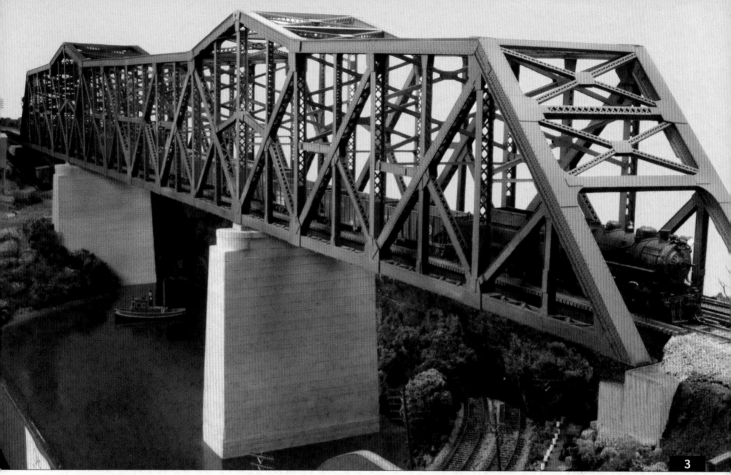

The Ohio River bridge at Steubenville, Ohio, is one of the signature structures on the part of the PRR that Bill Neale models. He discovered that the Atlas single-track O scale bridge made a great heavy-duty double-track bridge in HO with components large enough to match the prototype's 44"-square girders. Three bridges were needed to kitbash an 8-foot-long HO bridge. *Bill Neale*

a series of bents) inserted at the mid point, but this is a sure sign of an aging bridge or one that has to support much heavier loads than it was designed for – not a good situation in any event. This means that you need an end abutment or a supporting pier or tower at each end of every bridge segment.

(The exception is the cantilever bridge, which is essentially two independent bridges that meet in the middle, and each bridge half is designed to be self-supporting at its outer end. Some cantilever bridges support a relatively short through-truss bridge between the two cantilevered ends.)

A third rule of thumb is that gravity works downward. This means that there must be something directly under each end of each span of a bridge to hold it up. You can't simply butt the end of the bridge up against an abutment and hope it will stay there.

Ohio River bridge

One of the signature structures on the part of the Pennsylvania Railroad that

Bill Neale models in HO is the large double-track through-truss bridge at Steubenville, Ohio. He considered a number of alternatives for the basic construction material with little luck until he encountered a nice Atlas O scale through truss bridge at a local hobby shop. The O scale bridge had components large enough to match the prototype's massive 44"-square girders, and close inspection of this kit revealed that the rivets were very fine in size and could easily pass for HO scale large rivets.

Bill purchased three of the Atlas bridges and used their components to kitbash the major girders of a larger 8-foot-long HO bridge, **3**.

The Little Vermilion bridge

I described how I kitbashed a deck-girder bridge to span the Little Vermilion River valley in the November 2010 *Model Railroader*, but a brief review may prove helpful.

One of the most important design considerations for any kitbashing

project, and especially for deck-girder bridges supported by towers and bents, is the kit's tower height. The main source for towers and steel bents is Micro Engineering, which is what I used. Rather than trying to determine the exact height of the prototype bridge, I felt it was smarter to observe the overall structure of the bridge's towers and bents and then use stock kits parts to approximate them. In this case, the tower and bents were two "stories" high, whereas the kit has three stories or panels. So job one was to measure the height of the kit tower moldings with the bottom story cut off. I then made a scale drawing of the proposed bridge and attached it to the middle-deck roadbed to see how this fixed vertical depth would fit in the space I had reserved for it, **4**.

Fortunately, after allowing for the height of the girders, their concrete footings, and the ¾" plywood substructure, I found that I still had almost 3" of clearance for the tracks on the deck below the bridge scene,

These three photos show how a to-scale template of a deck-girder bridge I built using Micro Engineering and Central Valley components was employed to test-fit it both vertically and horizontally. By cutting the three-story towers and bent down to two, it cleared the NKP main line on the bottom deck yet still looked prototypical. Note the ¾" aluminum channel used as the core of the bridge.

4

which nicely cleared an NMRA standards gauge.

(You're probably thinking that a smarter approach would have been to design the railroad so as to ensure this clearance was achieved at the desired bridge location. You're correct; I lucked out.)

Also shown in **4** is the aluminum-channel core that I use for all deck-girder bridges. I got this idea from Jim Gaines, and it ensures a solid, level bridge deck from end to end. It requires the use of bridge girders that are high enough to cover the side of the channel while allowing enough room for the lower X-bracing that separates the two girders. You may find that the X-braces do not space the girders far enough apart to fit over the channel; adding small plastic tabs

to the ends of each X-brace solves this problem.

I didn't want to show the bridge as being freshly painted, so I sprayed it with Floquil Grimy Black and later brushed on a thick coat of Rust-All weathering solution. This will run down the sides (remember the gravity rule) and pool along the bottom flanges of the girders, just where rust would accumulate on a prototype bridge. So weathering takes about 10 seconds per bridge side!

I built several similar bridges for the Allegheny Midland. Where I needed to span longer distances, I used Central Valley's thicker (taller) girders, **5**.

Trestles

Railroad bridge engineers are a clever lot. They use materials economically

and find simple solutions to cope with everyday needs.

When I needed a wood pile trestle for the NKP main line and passing track just east of Veedersburg, Ind., I first considered ways to build bents that were wide enough to accommodate both tracks. But a civil-engineer friend reminded me that would not reflect good engineering practice, since damage to one bridge would probably take out both bridges at a time when the second bridge would be critically needed as a bypass. Maintenance could also be done on one trestle without affecting the other.

This was good news, as Walthers makes an excellent plastic kit for a wood-pile trestle (No. 933-3147). I bought two and staggered the bents to maintain 2" track center line spacing, **6**.

Longer spans require thicker girders to achieve the desired 7:1 length-to-height ratio. This bridge over the Coal Fork on the HO Allegheny Midland shows the mix of Central Valley and Micro Engineering girders.

Where two wood trestles are built side by side, as on the main and passing tracks at Veedersburg, Ind., on my NKP layout, they are built as separate structures to allow one to stay in service as the other is being repaired.

The "batter" or taper found on most bridge piers is readily visible on the pier supporting a curved-chord bridge (background) over the Wabash River east of Cayuga, Ind. The upstream side of this pier would also be cast into a wedge shape or "cutwater" to guide water and flood debris around the pier.

About abutments and piers...

As much as I appreciate innovation, too much of it is evident in many, perhaps most, commercially produced stone and concrete bridge abutments and piers. Rather than simply copying prototype examples, too often the manufacturers resort to their fanciful imagination as to how such structures look, and the results would not survive in the real world.

Look closely at a concrete pier or abutment and you'll notice that it gets wider toward the base. This taper or slope is called "batter," 7, and it's not there for aesthetics but rather is an important engineering consideration. So a pier or abutment that has perfectly vertical sides is unsuitable for a scale model of a bridge.

Concrete piers and abutments are poured into forms, and evidence of the boards or forms that create the desired shape is usually visible on the sides of the structure.

It's relatively easy to make concrete abutments or piers from plaster castings, solid wood blocks, styrene or ABS sheet, or even balsa. I usually make my abutments from ¼" balsa, "paint" them with a plaster slurry, and then coat them with a yellowish-tinged concrete color, 8. Older concrete may acquire a tan color, often the result of rust from iron particles in the aggregate or even an overhead steel structure washing down the concrete.

Doubling a covered bridge

Anyone who has modeled in any of the larger scales based on No. 1 gauge's 45mm track has come to realize just how enormous these models really are. Anything that we can do to save space is an avenue well worth exploring.

When I built a project railroad based on New Hampshire's Claremont & Concord for *Model Railroader* back in 2005, I wanted to include a signature scene that remained from part of this railroad's Boston & Maine days: the covered bridge over the Sugar River near Kellyville, N.H., 9. Fortunately, Aristo-Craft makes a similar covered bridge, so the main task was to double its length.

I couldn't devote enough layout length to accommodate two spans, so I trimmed off the roof overhang on one span and butted it up against a plastic "funhouse" mirror, which was trimmed to size and had a hole cut for the railroad at a local glass shop. The "middle" pier was made half the desired thickness and glued to the mirror. This technique could be used to virtually extend almost any bridge, especially where a railroad exits the scenicked portion of the layout.

Combinations

Chapter 8 is devoted to a single, relatively easy project: a combination depot plus interlocking tower based on an eye-catching prototype found on the Santa Fe. The project includes techniques you can use with many other kitbashing projects.

The unusual bridge abutments on both ends of the NKP bridge over the Little Vermillion River along the Indiana-Illinois state line are balsa covered with a light coating of wet plaster, then painted a warm tan or sand color to simulate aged concrete.

A two-span covered bridge for my Claremont & Concord 1:29 project railroad is actually a single Aristo-Craft span and half-width pier reflected in a plastic mirror. The mirror also serves to end the rural segment of the railroad; downtown Claremont is on the other side.

1

Combination tower and depot

I combined a Walthers Golden Valley Depot kit with a Walthers built-up interlocking tower. The current unavailability of the tower in kit form precluded swapping the front and rear walls to allow the tower to be positioned at the left end of the depot, thus more closely resembling the Santa Fe's Ottawa Junction combination depot and tower that inspired this project.

One photo can inspire a modeling project, 1. Published photos inspired many of the buildings on the Allegheny Midland. One Jim Boyd photo of QN Cabin (see Chapter 1) set the tone for all AM railroad structures. So let's explore that path by taking a hard look at not one but two photos of a combination depot and tower that graced the Santa Fe at Ottawa Junction, Kan., 2.

Homage to the Santa Fe

For those who like the basic look of the combination depot plus tower, a free-lanced model could easily be kitbashed. But let's go a bit beyond anything-goes and use the Ottawa Junction structure as our objective. What do we know about it?

Ottawa Junction was the subject of an article by then-editor Paul Larson in the August 1952 *Model Railroader*. But let's use this as a lesson in kitbashing by assuming we don't have copies of that article and therefore must proceed based on what we do know—which is what shows in the two photos at right.

Both sides face tracks, but the front has a bay window and truncated end where it butts against the tower. The tower has many second-story windows on both front and back walls. The entire building is covered with clapboard or novelty (shiplap) siding. There is a central chimney. A freight door is to the right of the bay window, but there is no "people door" on this side of the building or freight door in the back.

From these two photos, we know little about the end walls except that the top of the tower stairway is enclosed, probably as a buffer against the cold blasts of a Kansas winter. Without end-view photos or drawings, I'd be reluctant to scratchbuild a model of this building, but I wouldn't hesitate to kitbash a similar structure.

Two Walthers models—Golden Valley Depot (No. 933-2806) and interlocking tower (No. 933-2839)—can be kitbashed into a structure that has the same general attributes. Remember that kitbashing is not scratchbuilding: Compromises are part of the game plan.

One compromise is immediately evident: The two structures are not the same width, whereas the siding on the prototype is continuous from depot to tower on both front and rear. More obvious is the depot kit's different bay window. I didn't correct this, but one could replace the roof using Pikestuff shingled roof panels (No. 541-1007). I'd then extend the bay window sides up to a new peaked roof cut from a second set of these handy roof moldings.

These photos show the interesting combination depot and tower that served the Santa Fe at Ottawa Junction, Kan. It appears that the Santa Fe was an early adopter of the art of kitbashing two structures into one. If one is willing to overlook some features such as the continuous siding along the walls of the joined structures, it's not difficult to kitbash a reasonably close stand-in model. I had to reverse the position of the tower when I could not locate a tower kit and had to make do with a built-up model. Almost any depot and tower kits could be combined to model an interesting combination depot and tower. *Two photos: David P. Morgan Library collection*

2

Photo **3** shows the construction steps. I started with a built-up tower that was factory painted light gray with dark-gray trim. Since I wanted to re-use this tower in those colors on my NKP layout, I did not repaint it in Santa Fe's Colonial Yellow and Bronze Green with a Venetian Red roof.

For those who want to follow AT&SF practice for lineside structures, Keith Jordan supplied a copy of the Santa Fe Ry. Historical & Modeling Society's model paint recommendations, which were developed by Andy Sperandeo and Matt Zebrowski:
• Colonial Yellow (walls):
Polly Scale

170 UP Armour Yellow (1 part)
113 Reefer White (1 part)
Humbrol
074 Linen
• Bronze Green (trim):
Polly Scale
374 Southern Sylvan Green (1 part)
284 Pullman Green (1 part)
Humbrol
075 Bronze Green
• Venetian Red (roof):
Polly Scale
350 Mineral Red

"In my opinion, what really clinches the Santa Fe look are the white sashes," Andy said. "That cross-and-circle herald helps a lot too!"

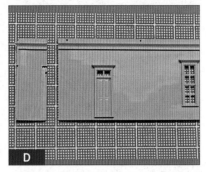
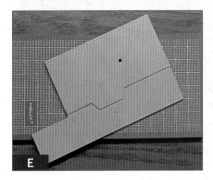

The front wall is shortened to the right of the left-hand window (A). The underlying base wall had to retain the beveled corner and hence was trimmed in two places (B). The front base wall then served as a pattern to cut a matching rear wall (C). The cut went through the freight door opening (D), but sheathing covered the joint. Flush-cutting pliers made quick work of projecting end-wall trim pieces (E). The floor was trimmed to fit the new front and rear walls (F). The rear-wall sheathing had to be spliced, and the irregular joint was covered with a strip of .010" x .100" styrene (G).

Since I was basing the model on the Ottawa Junction structure, I put the tower at one end of the depot, a relatively common practice on full-size railroads. It would have been only slightly more difficult to cut off most of the lower story of the tower so as to match the slope of the depot's roof and perch it midway stop the depot, like the C&O did for Quinnimont (see Chapter 1).

But a bit of "virtual kitbashing" done on my desktop computer using photo-editing software (see page 77) revealed a snag: I had a kit for the depot but only a built-up version of the tower (Walthers no longer offered the kit at this writing). Using the built-up tower gave me two choices:

1. To keep the steps intact, I had to turn the tower so that the chimney side faced the front of the depot, which didn't look good. If I had had a kit, I could have swapped the front and rear walls and quickly solved this problem, which is exactly what I would do if I were a Santa Fe modeler constructing a stand-in for Ottawa Junction. A check of a local hobby shop or an eBay search should prove fruitful.

2. I could put the tower on the right end of the depot. In either case, this isn't quite as easy as it may first seem, as—like the depot roof—the window trim on the left end of the tower and on the right end of the depot project out into harm's way. But it's not difficult to shorten the roof (on both ends) using a razor saw and to remove the offending trim work with flush-cutting pliers and a file.

Swapping ends with the tower resulted in the project drifting a little further away from the AT&SF prototype than I had initially contemplated. But as a freelanced kitbashing project, this worked fine, as the main goal was to show that even in this age of built-up structures, "kit"-bashing is not a lost art. In that respect, I think the project was a success.

A major lineside industry

Next: How about a soybean processing plant that I found lurking inside a cement plant kit's box? We'll discuss that project in Chapter 9.

3

Virtual kitbashing

Taking digital photos of models and combining and editing the images can be a great help in kitbashing, allowing you to virtually kitbash a model without picking up a hobby knife. Most cameras and computers come with photo-editing software. I prefer Adobe's Photoshop Elements. It's powerful but not expensive—it sells for less than $100.

For this project, I placed the tower next to an Atlas Maywood depot I had on hand and shot a photo (top). Using Elements, I erased the left end of the depot to shorten it, then used the rubber stamp (clone) tool to recopy the depot portion of the image so that it abutted the tower. Touching up the interface was done using the clone and paintbrush tools.

To correct the color mismatch, I used the Enhance > Adjust Color > Replace Color tools to change the buff and brown to two colors of gray. This same tool would have

allowed me to "repaint" the tower and depot into any color scheme to see how it would look. This can be especially helpful for a freelancer who is trying to decide on a railroad structure color scheme.

The new image showed several concerns: The siding on the depot and tower didn't match, which prompted me to dig out the Valley Depot kit I actually used, and the chimney on the bay-window side of the structure really looked out of place. If I had had a tower kit rather than the built-up version, I could have swapped the front and rear walls to correct the latter concern.

The altered photo also showed that the tower windows facing the depot roof would have to be shortened. Kit builders could simply swap a piece of Evergreen siding for the visible part of this wall.

1

CHAPTER NINE

From cement to soybean plant

I kitbashed this version of the Frankfort soybean plant for my Nickel Plate Road HO scale layout.

Just west of the former New York, Chicago & St. Louis (Nickel Plate Road) yard at Frankfort, Ind., stands a towering concrete edifice that at first glance looks like a grain elevator. It's actually a soybean processing plant, built by Swift & Co. in 1946 to convert soybeans into bean meal, "cake," and oil, which are used for a vast array of products. The Swift plant was purchased by A.E. Staley in the late 1970s, and ADM bought the plant in 1985. It's still doing a booming business and may soon be expanded once again.

This chapter is reprinted from *How to Build Realistic Layouts: Industries You Can Model*, a special 2007 issue of *Model Railroader*.

A soybean processing plant, such as this one in Frankfort, Ind., is a great traffic-generating industry. *George Jay Morris, John B. Corns collection*

Beans, then as now, arrived by rail. In 1962, for example, recently retired NKP (and subsequent Norfolk & Western/Norfolk Southern) engineer Don Daily reported that 2,247 loads came from elevators on the NKP. The Pennsylvania and Monon railroads, which crossed the NKP near the center of Frankfort, added another 2,095 and 305 loads, respectively. Outbound loads totaled 3,534 routed over the NKP and another 2,698 to the PRR and 155 to the Monon. On average, the

NKP delivered about six loaded Swift cars per day to the PRR interchange and a Swift load every other day to the Monon.

Bean oil was shipped out in tank cars, just as it is today. The meal was shipped in boxcars, often in bags, but today it's shipped in covered hoppers. Hexane or naptha is used to extract soybean oil from the bean hulls after they have been crushed into flakes. Until the late 1950s, coal for the boiler house (long since dismantled), used to

make steam to increase the moisture content of the bean meal, was shipped into the plant. The boilers were later fueled with oil.

Mark E. Vaughan, who worked for Central Soya, reports that some soybean plants he worked at received occasional carloads of kaolin (white clay used to make porcelain plumbing fixtures and to coat enameled paper) to add to the meal to improve flowability. It usually came in Southern jumbo covered hoppers (1960 and later).

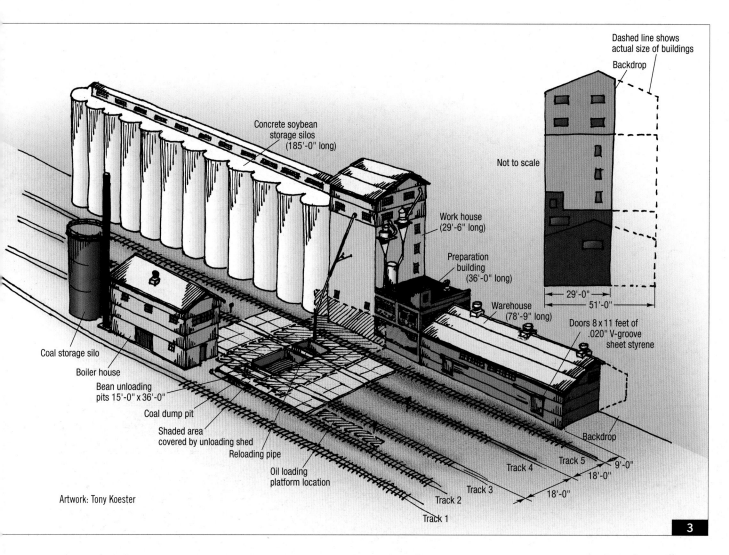

Concrete soybean
storage silos
(185'-0" long)

Work house
(29'-6" long)

Preparation
building
(36'-0" long)

Warehouse
(78'-9" long)

Coal storage silo

Boiler house

Bean unloading
pits 15'-0" x 36'-0"

Coal dump pit

Shaded area
covered by unloading shed

Reloading pipe

Oil loading
platform location

Track 1

Track 2

Track 3

Track 4

Track 5

Dashed line shows
actual size of buildings

Backdrop

Not to scale

29'-0"

51'-0"

Doors 8 x 11 feet of
.020" V-groove
sheet styrene

Backdrop

9'-0"

18'-0"

18'-0"

Artwork: Tony Koester

3

He also recalls soybean flakes being shipped in 40-foot boxcars for use in animal feed.

When the Frankfort plant was built just north of the NKP's Peoria Division main line, the old main became boxcar and tank car storage track 1, and a new main was built to skirt around the bean plant farther to the south. (See the aerial photo on page 84.) The plant was originally switched from both ends, as there was a lead out of the NKP's westbound yard into the plant as well as a connection at the west end to the Peoria Division main. For switching information, see "Bean-plant traffic" on page 83.

Modeling the bean plant

This is the largest industry on my HO railroad, which depicts the eastern half of the NKP's St. Louis Division, as well as a short stretch of the Peoria Division, as they appeared in the 1950s.

The bean plant's varied traffic and imposing-yet-manageable size make it a good modeling candidate for almost any railroad set in the granger (agricultural) belt.

The Swift plant comprises several separate buildings, but I was concerned only with the structures on the track side, as my bean plant butts up against the backdrop. The warehouse at the east end of the complex is 50 x 80 feet, but I had only a scale 29 feet of width to work in. Rather than change the end-view proportions by narrowing that building or the adjacent preparation building and tall work house, I truncated the north side.

The prototype has two rows of 13 silos, each 23 feet in diameter. The row of silos is 322 feet long and 106 feet high. That's a bit generous even for my basement-size layout. Moreover, I hoped to find a suitable kitbashing "donor" to save time. So I selectively

compressed the storage silos' height and length.

As I paged through the Walthers HO catalog in hopes of finding corrugated-metal buildings for the warehouse and top of the workhouse, I discovered that my bean plant was actually hiding inside a Walthers box labeled "Valley Cement." This plastic kit includes not only an eight-silo complex (two rows of four) but also several corrugated metal outbuildings.

Since only the front row of silos is readily visible from the track (south) side, I built the model in partial relief against the backdrop, unfolding the kit's front and rear silo shells into one long row of eight silos to create a reasonable suggestion of the prototype's massive appearance. The silos are essentially identical to those in the Walthers ADM elevator kit, so I used an additional four-silo front wall section from that kit to extend my

This photo of the expanded Frankfort, Ind., plant is from the early 1970s. Notice that there are more tanks and piping than shown in the 1946 photo on page 79.

complex to within one row of silos of the prototype. I kitbashed the conveyor shed that runs along the top of the silos from parts in the Valley Cement kit plus some Evergreen .040" styrene metal siding.

Only the lower portions of the tall work house and abutting preparation building had to be scratchbuilt. Their box-like structure made this a simple project using Evergreen and Plastruct .040" styrene sheet. I used a nibbling tool, available at RadioShack or through Micro-Mark, to rough-cut window and door openings, then filed them to the final opening dimensions using a small mill file.

I initially thought the preparation building was solid concrete. However, I recalled seeing a photo of it on the cover of John B. Corns' book, *Nickel Plate Road Publicity Photos 1943-1952, Vol. 2,* taken in the 1940s. It shows that this building had concrete posts and beams and brick curtain walls. I simulated this look on my model by masking off the concrete parts and then rubbing Bragdon Enterprises aging chalks into the brick areas in horizontal strokes. Adding thin styrene pilasters would have achieved more of a 3-D effect.

The "Soybean Road"

The November 1949 issue of the *Nickel Plate Road Magazine* observed that during the fall harvest, the NKP "could well be called the 'Soybean Road.'" More than 37 percent of all the soybeans produced in the United States were grown within 25 miles of the NKP, the report stated, and in 1948 the railroad carried 7,500 carloads of soybeans and another 6,500 loads of soybean products: oil, cake, and meal. Illinois was the leading soybean state in the nation, growing more than a third of the nation's total production at the end of the 1940s. Two other states served by the NKP, Indiana and Ohio, ranked third and fourth.

In 1949, the harvest began in mid-September, with carloads of beans moving to online processing plants in Chicago, Peoria, East St. Louis, Bloomington, and Gibson City in Illinois; Lafayette, Portland, and Frankfort, Ind.; and Delphos, Fostoria, Toledo, Bellevue, and Painesville, Ohio. The article reported that inbound bean shipments were expected to continue to be heavy through the end of November.

As is evident from the Frankfort bean plant I built for my railroad, most of the beans are stored in silos. Processing the soybeans—separating the meal and oil by crushing or by a chemical process—is a year-round operation. The NKP and other granger roads moved shipments from the bean plants during every month of the year. Beans shipped in were occasionally shipped back out if the plant was filled to capacity.

Soybeans first came to North America in 1804 but garnered little attention. Prior to 1935, soybean oil was used primarily in soaps, paints, and varnishes. During the 1930s and '40s, soybeans became the number two cash crop in the Corn Belt. By then, bean oil was used in edible products such as vegetable shortening, margarine, cooking and salad oils, and mayonnaise. Industrial uses run from resins and rubber substitutes to linoleum and printing ink. The meal and hulls, rich in protein, are used as feed for animals and poultry, as well as in fertilizer, adhesives, and paper coatings.

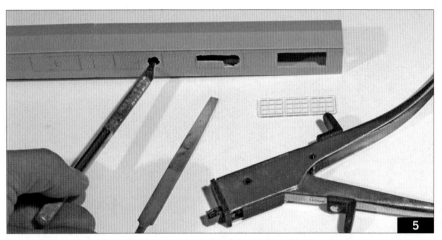

To make window openings, I bored a starting hole with a hobby knife blade and then cut out the plastic with a nibbling tool (right). I then used a small mill file (middle) to finish the edges and square the corners.

The unloading pit walls are stacked .060" x .100" styrene strips. The pits and the surrounding concrete pad were airbrushed with Model Master Camouflage Gray paint. The concrete base is .040" sheet styrene.

This view of the plant's west end shows the bean storage silos, coal storage silo with elevator, smokestack, and powerhouse. I used Bragdon Enterprises aging powders to simulate the pour marks on the concrete silos.

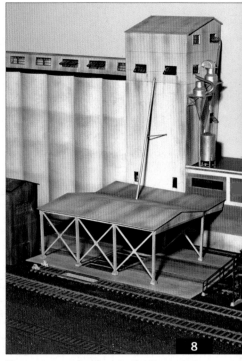

The soybean unloading shed at the end of the complex was kitbashed from corrugated siding and supports from the Walthers coal mine kit.

The windows for my plant came from the Valley Cement kit and several Walthers New River coal preparation plant kits, but you could substitute other commercial window moldings. I trimmed and cemented a few of the windows so that they were in the open position for visual interest.

The Swift plant also had an unloading shed and a boiler house. I used leftover wall parts from the cement plant and .040"-spaced corrugated-metal siding stock from Evergreen to fill in gaps when I ran short. The boiler house had to be narrowed considerably to fit my limited space.

I used a length of K&S ½" brass tubing for the smokestack and painted it and the boiler house flat black. I weathered this structure with Bragdon Enterprises aging powders.

I built the 15 x 36-foot unloading pits by stacking .060" x .100" styrene strips. I embedded the pits in the layout's Homasote roadbed and then extended the pit walls high enough to support the rails of the two unloading tracks as they bridged the openings.

The bean oil loading dock doesn't show in any photos I've seen. One

Bean-plant traffic

In the 1940s and '50s, inbound traffic to the bean plant was primarily 40-foot boxcars filled with soybeans from grain elevators along the line. They were unloaded over the pit on tracks 3 and 4. The plant also received an occasional load of coal for the powerhouse, spotted on track 2, and hexane (used to extract bean meal) in tank cars spotted at the west end of track 5.

According to documents from 1948-50 salvaged by Don Daily and compiled by Bill Darnaby, a typical day saw the NKP pull four boxcars loaded with bean meal, often in 100-pound bags, from track 5 and one or two tank cars filled with bean oil from track 2. Traffic could be much heavier during the September to November bean rush, so the NKP often called a second engine crew around 2:30 p.m. to switch the plant until the regular 10:30 p.m. industrial engine crew came on duty.

Jerry Cory, who began work at Swift in 1955, recalls using a Trackmobile to switch the plant. A bulldozer and front-end loader were also used to move cars around on occasion. In 1976 the plant got a Plymouth diesel, and Jerry said that it was used to move empty boxcars to a clean-out area where additional beans were retrieved from the "empty" cars by a private crew, which also cleaned and prepared the boxcars for meal loading.

Routings did not seem to be strictly toward each car's home road. For example, a Santa Fe boxcar loaded with bean meal was routed NKP-PRR-Baltimore & Ohio on January 6, 1948. Most bean meal loads were headed to nearby Midwestern cities via the NKP, PRR, New York Central, Illinois Central, Milwaukee Road (via its Southeastern line, which extended into the southern Indiana coalfields), or Monon, or farther east to destinations on the B&O, Chesapeake & Ohio, and even the Long Island and Central Vermont, the latter via Canada.

Soybean plants generate a lot of traffic, making them a busy place for railroad switching work. *George Jay Morris photo, John B. Corns collection*

Tank cars carrying soybean oil were privately owned, however, so they could be routed to any destination without concern for trying to head them toward a home road. Loading records frequently show General American Transportation Corp. (GATX reporting marks), North American Car Corp. (NATX), Shippers Car Line Corp. (SHPX), and Union Tank Car Co. (UTLX) tank cars loaded with bean oil. Destinations include the East Coast (NKP-Lackawanna-Jersey Central or NKP-PRR-Susquehanna, for example) and Appalachia (NKP-C&O-Southern or NKP-Big Four-N&W—Big Four is the New York Central's Cleveland, Cincinnati, Chicago & St. Louis Ry.). A frequent customer for bean oil was another Swift operation in Atlanta, Ga.

---

report noted there were "steps up to the top of the tank cars and a boom that was lowered to the domes." I kitbashed the dock from a Walthers oil unloading platform, using only one delivery pipe and loading crane to load one tank car at a time.

How hexane was unloaded at the west end of track 5 is equally unclear. Jerry Cory, who worked at the Frankfort plant, recalls a hose being connected to the top of the dome, which is normal for pressurized tank cars. Photos of similar installations are shown in figs. 2-11 and 2-18 of Jeff Wilson's *The Model Railroader's Guide to Industries Along the Tracks* (Kalmbach Books). A Woodland Scenics diesel-fuel crane could be used for this.

Painting and weathering

I spray-painted the concrete parts of the structure with Floquil Concrete, but it looked too dark for this application. I then oversprayed a "highlight" coat of Model Master Camouflage Gray, which is actually almost tan, leaving some of the darker color in the recesses to add depth.

It's important to add some "texture" to the smooth-plastic silos to simulate the horizontal banding that results as concrete is poured into forms; it's clearly visible in the photo I shot in 1971. I did this by wrapping the silos with masking tape just above each pour mark, starting at the bottom, and using a stiff brush to apply Bragdon Enterprises aging powders.

I also applied some warmer rust colors along with a bit of soot. The masking tape made the pour divisions a bit too sharp, however, so after removing the tape, I scrubbed the lines with gray powder (ash) to blur them somewhat.

The SWIFT lettering evident in later years does not appear in the steam-era photo that John Corns supplied, so I didn't include it. A post-1985 version of this bean plant would be lettered for ADM.

The corrugated metal surfaces got a coat of flat aluminum, but they looked too new and shiny, so I resprayed them with Floquil Primer. I used Bragdon aging powders to show some rust and soot here and there.

Car fleets

For my 1950s-era layout, almost any 40-foot boxcar in good condition is suitable for inbound beans and outbound loads of bean meal. Before the boxcars could be loaded, however, they had to be cleaned, and there was a clean-out track right on the Swift property at Frankfort for that purpose. The NKP had to switch the cars in and out of this track, so it serves as a separate industry in that sense.

Loaded cars were weighed on the scale track on the east lead into the plant. The scale location suggests that loads of soybeans were shoved into the plant from the east side and empties were retrieved from the west lead.

The pipe angling down from the top of the head house was used to reload excess beans into boxcars on track 4 over the unloading pit for reshipment to other plants.

Today, ADM continues to receive soybeans and hexane by rail. It occasionally uses lime for meal flowability. Bean meal is shipped in covered hoppers and bean oil in tank cars.

A recent aerial view of the ADM (former Swift) plant at Frankfort shows the relocated NKP (Norfolk Southern) main to Peoria at far left. Stub-ended sidings now serve the plant, and there are many structure changes, such as the addition of the large white storage bins.
John Brill photo, Don Daily collection

Close enough

The bean plant project consumed about a week of modeling time. Although the resulting model isn't an exact replica of its prototype, I think it captures the massiveness, overall proportions, and appearance of the original well.

There was a scale track and house on the east lead into the soybean plant, but I haven't seen a photo of the scale house taken in the steam era. For now, I plan to use Walthers' new scale house kit.

Last, a note of appreciation: Unraveling what happened within the bean plant trackage was greatly aided by John B. Corns, Jerry Cory, retired NKP engineer Don Daily, tank car authority Tony Thompson, and Mark Vaughan.

Grain doors

When boxcars were the primary carrier of corn, wheat, and soybeans, several methods were used to keep these products inside the car during transit and when the doors were opened at the destination. The most common was the grain door, which was actually a stack of panels, each three boards high, nailed inside the boxcar door from the bottom sill to within a couple of feet from the top of the door.

Cheaper cardboard door liners were later substituted for the wood doors with mixed results; tears resulted in substantial leakage. Grain inspectors had to open doors and were not amused if the liner had ripped and they were buried in grain or beans.

Grain doors were tracked like boxcars, as the railroads expected to get them back for reuse or salvage. Most were stenciled with the reporting marks of the owning railroad, as shown in the accompanying photo by Willis McCaleb on the cover of the July-August 1952 NKP company magazine. They were typically held at a major unloading site, such as the Swift bean plant in Frankfort, until a carload of them was ready to be interchanged to the owning railroad.

Model grain doors or liners are available from Modeler's Choice, Sunshine Models, and Jaeger HO Products.

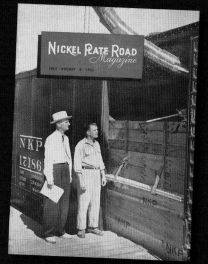

Railroads expected to get their grain doors back after use, so they were stenciled with the railroad's name, like those for the NKP shown here.

Working car puller for your soybean plant

At a prototype bean plant, loaded cars of beans are moved over a pit, unloaded, and moved off the pit (usually with a car puller) so the next car can be unloaded. From a modeling perspective, how do you know when a car has been unloaded? My solution was to create a mechanism that actually moved cuts of cars through the unloading shed. Once through, the cars would then be considered empty and ready to be taken away for cleaning. I devised a simple car puller using a Hankscraft display motor, fishing line, and a dummy coupler.

To start, I timed how long it took for the Hankscraft motor to make one revolution at 10 volts, but with enough added resistance to slow it down so that it would barely move without stalling. Once I knew the motor speed, I calculated the radius of a pulley wheel needed to advance the cars at a rate of one car per 15 fast-time minutes. (It takes 90 fast minutes to unload a six-car cut of boxcars, which is about 30 actual minutes.)

I made the pulleys for each motor from two .060"-thick styrene disks. Each disk is cut with a small chamfer, and when the disks are placed back to back, they form a pulley with a groove deep enough to guide fishing line. I drilled the center of the pulleys to fit the motor shaft tightly, but I also secured them with cyanoacrylate adhesive (CA).

The motors are mounted directly under each track, approximately at the unloading pit. The tow line (nylon fishing line) wraps once around the pulley, and one end attaches to a lead fishing weight, creating constant tension on the line. The other end of the line runs from the motor under the layout to the end of the track. It then passes through the scenery inside a length of brass tubing bent at a 90-degree angle at the top.

To firmly anchor the lines at the ends of the tracks at coupler height, I set the brass tubing into simulated concrete bases made from styrene. These bases, intended to look like heavy bumper stops, are glued to the layout and absorb the tension in the line.

The end of the line is tied to a brass dummy coupler. I filed the coupler's knuckles to easily drop into a Kadee No. 5 coupler. I also soldered a piece of .020" brass wire along the length of the dummy coupler and across the top of the knuckle opening. The wire keeps the dummy coupler from slipping out of the regular car couplers.

An operator starts the sequence by positioning a cut of six or fewer cars on the unloading track with the first car in the unloading shed. He then slips the dummy coupler over that car's coupler and throws the toggle switch to activate the puller. The motor pulls the cut along at the rate of one car every 15 fast minutes, and when it reaches the end of the track, the puller simply stalls. The operator can then shut off the motor when it's convenient, lift the dummy coupler from the end car and pull the cut of cars to the cleanout track with a locomotive. If more loaded cars are waiting, the operator has the option of pulling the dummy

To pass easily through the layout, Bill Darnaby threaded the line through a brass tube. *Three photos: Bill Darnaby*

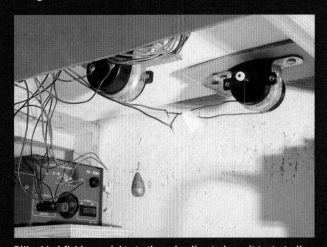

Bill added fishing weights to the nylon line to keep it taut at all times. Hankscraft display motors do the pulling.

The line attaches to a cut of cars, using a brass dummy coupler modified to stay seated in a knuckle coupler.

coupler and line back to the starting point by hand and running another cut of cars through the unloader. To allow this, the toggle switches have a position to run the motors backwards at a much higher speed than when pulling.
– Bill Darnaby

1

CHAPTER TEN

Kitbashing cornucopia

Paul Dolkos made several subtle modifications to the **HO Atlas Middlesex Manufacturing Co. kit** on the left. He positioned the far end wall diagonally to fit the space, built more conventional entrance steps of styrene, and added a small loading dock on the side. Although Paul noted that "the long front and back walls were not molded to be easily changed," he managed to swap them better to fit the location. A major change was the scratchbuilt addition on the right, which reflects a later period of industrial architecture. Paul also added downspouts to both structures and "painted" signs from homemade decals. The smokestack is a Vollmer kit. *Paul Dolkos*

Before reading the captions that accompany the ensuing examples of the kitbashing art by a variety of skilled model builders, try to guess which kit(s) went into their assembly. If you can't, that's good—one of the primary objectives of kitbashing has been met. Then ask yourself how the builder managed to disguise the original kit's heritage—wider or taller, a new type of roof, a new purpose, backdating or modernization, maybe only a new coat of paint—and why he may have chosen to do that.

White Mountain Paper, another kitbashed HO scale structure by Paul Dolkos (also see page 57), is a modification of the City Classics Smallman Street warehouse. Many modelers increase the building's height with the firm's add-on kit, but Paul removed one of kit's three stories and added additional sections to increase the length and width. The longer, lower footprint seemed more appropriate in the rural mill setting. He also added a loading dock and canopy on two sides and bricked over some window openings. *Paul Dolkos*

The Wissota Furniture Co. is a Walthers REA Express building modified to fit into a corner of Gerry Leone's HO layout. The rear walls were used for the perpendicular addition. Gerry eliminated one railcar bay near the inside corner on the long side, as there'd be no way a boxcar could get back into that corner. The water tank is scratchbuilt from a panty-hose container and "some other stuff." He also modified most of the windows so they appear to be open. *Gerry Leone*

Veteran modelers should have little trouble recognizing the roots of this clever adaptation of the Revell HO enginehouse kit, later re-issued by Con-Cor. The basic kit was also marketed (with different end walls) as the Superior Bakery and a print shop. Gerry Leone stacked walls beside and atop the others to create a car-repair facility, where he stores his Masonite track-cleaning cars. Gerry said the light coming through the skylights and the huge windows necessitated detailing the second-floor interior. *Gerry Leone*

Gees Potato Chips started out as an HO Walthers Golden Valley Canning kit. Builder Gerry Leone admits that there is no rear or back to the building—he shortened the main part of the structure by one panel and used the back as the front long side of the one-story portion. The rear "peaked" side was cut down to one story and used as the front peaked side. The pipes are sprues and other miscellany. *Two photos: Gerry Leone*

Gerry Leone cut one story from an HO scale Bachmann Department Store to model a store more suited for a small Midwestern town. It butts up against a curved backdrop, so it has a triangular footprint. A Walthers fire escape adds some texture. *Gerry Leone*

Gerry Leone left the rear wall off of an HO scale DPM Cutting's Scissors kit at the edge of the layout to reveal the interior of the Hunt Paint store. Detailing the interior required figuring out where all the architectural elements such as stairways would go, adding interior window frames, and putting in support beams. *Gerry Leone*

Cliff Powers kitbashed this HO model of the J.J. Hechinger Bag & Burlap Co. from a Blair Line Backdrop Warehouse craftsman kit and a Model Tech Studios Seeley Milling kit. "I thought a craftsman-style kitbash might add some variety," Cliff said. *Cliff Powers*

Another large kitbashed structure by Cliff Powers, the Underwood Glass Bottle Co., was built from two Atlas HO Middlesex Manufacturing kits and four Walthers vintage fire escape kits. *Cliff Powers*

Cliff Powers' model of the Irby Cigar and Tobacco Co. began as four HO Walthers Fireproof Storage kits. He used the ground floor from two walls to add two extra stories to the remaining structure. *Cliff Powers*

One of the less-complicated projects by Cliff Powers is the Central Ice and Cold Storage Company, a kitbash of two Walthers HO scale R.J. Frost kits. *Cliff Powers*

Cliff Powers kitbashed the massive New Orleans Public Grain Elevator from four Walthers Red Wing Milling kits, numerous City Classics wall sections, and PVC pipe. Trains are routed behind the silos to enter a hidden five-track staging yard. *Cliff Powers*

₁₃

Cliff Powers kitbashed the 8-foot-long Napoleon Street Wharf warehouse from three Walthers Rolling Mills kits. A hidden five-track staging yard is accessed via a removable roof. The riverboat is an Artesania Latina kit; Cliff added two smoke generators! *Cliff Powers*

"When I build structures for my N scale Moffat Road," Mike Danneman reported, "I strive to create the look or feel of a prototype structure. This can be achieved either by building it from scratch or using commercially available kits to speed up the process." For structures in the snowbound town of Pinecliffe, Colo., Mike used several commercial stock kits that adequately "captured the feel" of the prototypes. But when it came to the post office, a signature building, he chose to kitbash it. The sloping roofline of the post office pointed him to JL Innovative Design's Sawpit Store (No. 320). The actual garage has two stalls, but the single-car garage that came with the kit better fit the available space. In the Rio Grande days, the building was also a small grocery store, so Mike added custom signs he made on his computer. The prototype photo is from January 31, 2012, and the building now has new siding and windows, solar panels, a satellite dish, and other details. *Two photos: Mike Danneman*

₁₄

One of my all-time favorite kitbashes is Allen McClelland's modification of the popular Atlas interlocking tower. Allen added a third story and lots of details; it stood guard at the hump yard at Jimtown, Va., on his original HO Virginian & Ohio layout. Both the first and second editions of the V&O are now history, but a section of the V&O has been added to Gerry Albers' Virginian Ry. A similar two-story tower that guarded a diamond crossing at Jimtown has found a new home—but apparently not a new job.
Two photos: Allen McClelland

Allen McClelland kitbashed these three small structures that now grace the V&O section of Gerry Albers' HO Virginian Ry. layout. The Fishing Supplies shanty is a Blair Line kit that Allen shortened. He combined the two buildings in JL Innovative Design's yard equipment kit into Reece Creations, maker of custom wood products. Big Joe's Plumbing is an Al Boos Bronco Models blacksmith shop kit with a new roof and front door. *Three photos: Gerry Albers*

16

Long-time Rock Island modeler Steve Hile is kitbashing this coaling station for his HO scale layout from a pair of Walthers No. 933-2922 Wood Coaling Tower kits plus an upper superstructure made from Evergreen styrene sheets. *Steve Hile*

About the author

How to Kitbash Structures is Tony Koester's tenth book focusing on his life-long hobby of model railroading. Tony has been the editor of *Model Railroad Planning*, a special annual issue of *Model Railroader* magazine, since its inception in 1995. He is a contributing editor to MR and writes the popular Trains of Thought column and numerous feature articles. He served as the editor of *Railroad Model Craftsman* magazine until joining Bell Laboratories in 1981. In 2001, he retired from a 20-year career in the telecommunications industry, where he was a technical writer, award-winning corporate science magazine and newspaper editor, corporate communications director, and anchor of the corporate television network.

Tony spent a quarter of a century designing, building, and with his friends operating the freelanced, coal-hauling Allegheny Midland—the Midland Road. More recently, he has been hard at work on a multi-deck HO railroad that accurately depicts the Nickel Plate Road's St. Louis Division as it appeared in 1954 and, like the AM, provided kitbashing projects that he incorporated into this book.

Acknowledgements

Special thanks to those who provided information and photos, including Gerry Albers, Jim Boyd, Jack Burgess, Art Curren, Don Daily, Dennis Daniels, Mike Danneman, Bill Darnaby, Paul Dolkos, Dave Frary, Steve Hile, Tom Johnson, Gerry Leone, Allen McClelland, Don McFall, Charlotte Miller, D.J. Mulhearn, Bill Neale, Ted Pamperin, Cliff Powers, and Doug Tagsold. Special thanks go to Jeff Wilson and his Kalmbach Books' boss, Dianne Wheeler, who once again guided my book through Kalmbach's meticulous production process.
Tony Koester
Newton, N.J.
April 2012

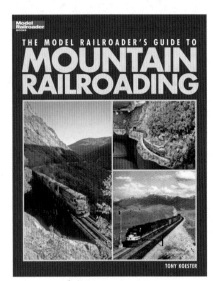
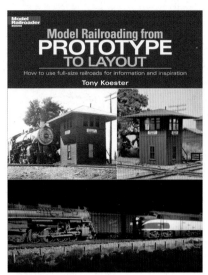
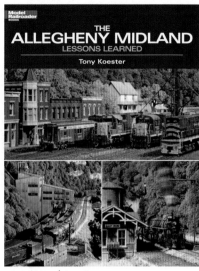